SPOOKY
New England

Tales of Hauntings, Strange Happenings,
and Other Local Lore

RETOLD BY S. E. SCHLOSSER

ILLUSTRATED BY PAUL G. HOFFMAN

Globe Pequot

GUILFORD, CONNECTICUT

For my dad—David Schlosser—who read me stories when I was little.

For my family, who threatened to tar and feather me if I did not mention them all by name: David, Dena, Tim, Arlene, Hannah, Emma, Nathan, Ben, Deb, Gabe, Clare, Jack, Chris, Karen, Davey, and Aunt Millie.

(See, Mom, I told you I would write a book someday.)

For Paul Hoffman and the fabulous folks at Globe Pequot Press, with my thanks.

* * *

Globe Pequot

An imprint of Rowman & Littlefield

Distributed by NATIONAL BOOK NETWORK

Copyright © 2017 by S. E. Schlosser

Illustrations copyright © 2017 Paul G. Hoffman

British Library Cataloguing in Publication Information available

Library of Congress Cataloging-in-Publication Data available

ISBN 978-1-4930-2712-5 (paperback)

ISBN 978-1-4930-2797-2 (ebook)

∞™ The paper used in this publication meets the minimum requirements of American National Standard for Information Sciences—Permanence of Paper for Printed Library Materials, ANSI/NISO Z39.48-1992.

Contents

PART TWO: POWERS OF DARKNESS AND LIGHT

Spooky Sites . . .

and where to find them

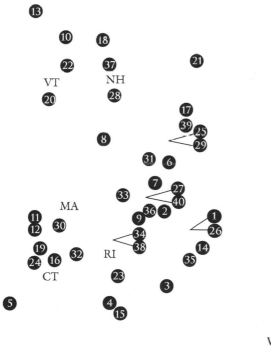

ME

VT

NH

MA

RI

CT

N

W ✦ E

S

Introduction

On a recent trip to England, I stayed at Apsley House Hotel in Bath, which was built by the Duke of Wellington for his mistress. It is said that the ghost of the duke occasionally glides through the walls, presumably to visit the residents of the house for *auld lang syne*. My room was comfortable and the bed very soft, so if the duke visited me at night, I was blissfully unaware of the whole thing. Perhaps now would be a good time to confess that it would take a poltergeist with a bucket of water and a two-by-four to waken me from my slumbers, so a gentleman like the duke probably had no chance. Still, I was a bit disappointed by my lack of a ghostly encounter.

I noticed on my trip that England seemed to be full of ghosts and mysterious tales dating back hundreds of years. In comparing England to America, I became conscious of a difference in the attitude toward folklore. While many of the older tales of ghosts, witches, and things that go bump in the night are well remembered by the people of England, the older, spooky tales of New England are rapidly disappearing from the memories of all but a few.

Take your average New England schoolchildren. They will probably have heard about Paul Bunyan; after all, Paul was born in Bangor, Maine (although the folks of Bemidji, Minnesota, still dispute this fact). I am sure that the average New England grandparent still remembers the five giant storks it took to deliver Paul to his parents, not to mention the tidal waves Paul caused when he turned over in his cradle—a raft built by his parents and floated off the coast of Maine.

But try asking the same kids if they have heard of Black Sam Bellamy, and they will probably think he's a character in the latest television cartoon series (the one they have to miss because of soccer practice).

So the old stories told around the fireplace on a long winter's evening are disappearing, replaced by television, movies, and computer games. Much of our folklore heritage is in danger of becoming lost to the general public. In its place arise stories of alligators in the sewers, "breathing" cacti, and George Turklebaum (he died at work, and it took five days for his colleagues to notice he was dead).

Although these new folktales deserve a place in our culture, it would be a tragedy to lose the rich folklore from our past. With this in mind, I have included several stories in *Spooky New England* that date back to the colonial and Revolutionary War periods. Twentieth-century spooks like the drowned sailor in "The Telltale Seaweed" and the friendly (or is he?) "Black Dog of Hanging Hills" rub shoulders with the "Watcher of the Isles of Shoals" and "Old Trickey," ghosts who have haunted the coast of New England for more than 200 years.

The next time you find yourself sitting around a campfire listening to someone tell the old chestnut about the girl who goes to bed in the dark because she doesn't want to disturb her roommate, then awakens to find her roommate dead and a bloody message scrawled on the wall ("Aren't you glad you didn't turn on the light?"), you can pull out your well-worn copy of *Spooky New England* and scare the living daylights out of your friends with the story of "Tom Dunn's Dance" or "The Loup-Garou." And if your group happens to be roasting marshmallows and drinking hot cocoa while enjoying this campfire, be sure to save me a seat!

—Sandy Schlosser

PART ONE
Ghost Stories

1

The Telltale Seaweed

PROVINCETOWN, MASSACHUSETTS

The rain was beating down on the windshield so hard that Elizabeth could hardly see the narrow Cape Cod road on which she was driving. It was nearly midnight. After spending the day sightseeing in Provincetown, she and her sister Patricia had joined acquaintances in the area for a leisurely dinner. It was after ten before they started back to the inn where they were spending their vacation. The storm had blown inland a few minutes after they'd left the restaurant.

The headlights were almost useless against the stormy darkness. A gust of wind made the old Ford shake violently. A flash of lightning briefly lit up the scraggly trees growing close to the road. The crash of thunder that immediately followed made Elizabeth jump.

"Maybe we should pull over until the storm lets up," suggested her sister nervously. Elizabeth glanced over, but all she could see of her petite, brunette sister was her silhouette. Patricia had always been frightened by storms.

They were driving along a particularly desolate part of the road. The trees were thick right up to the pavement. The rain and the dim headlights made everything seem spooky.

"I'd rather wait until we reached someplace more . . . populated," Elizabeth said.

At that moment the engine gave a violent knocking sound. The car shook with something more than the wind and then stalled right in the middle of the road.

"Please say we didn't just break down," said Patricia.

Elizabeth tried to restart the car several times but the engine wouldn't turn over.

"We're stuck," Patricia answered herself. "What are we going to do?"

"We'll have to find a house and phone someone to give us a tow," her sister said.

"Do you want me to wait with the car?" Patricia asked in a scared voice. Then the wind gave a giant gust and something slammed into the back windshield. The women both screamed as glass shattered under the weight of a large branch. Wind and rain came whipping into the car through the gaping hole, only partially plugged by the enormous limb.

"Are you all right?" Elizabeth asked shakily. Her sister nodded. The high seats in the front had protected them from most of the glass. "Well, that settles it. We can't stay here with that hole in the back windshield," Elizabeth continued. "We'll have to find someplace to stay for the night."

Taking a flashlight from under the seat, the two sisters ventured out into the storm. They were immediately soaked to the skin, and the roaring of the wind made talk impossible. After they'd walked for about five minutes, a flash of lightning revealed a waist-high stone wall that surrounded an overgrown lawn. Another flash seconds later showed an old, neglected-looking house set back a little way from the road.

"No!" Patricia shouted immediately over the wind. "We are not going in there."

"Do we have a choice?" Elizabeth yelled back. "We'll catch pneumonia if we stay out here any longer!"

She hurried up to the wall and walked along it until she came to an iron gate. The gate opened with a high-pitched groan. Elizabeth hesitated. The sound gave her goose bumps. Maybe Patricia was right. Maybe they should look for another place to stay.

Just then a fierce gust of wind drove the rain right into her eyes, and Elizabeth decided she was going to look no farther. She straightened her shoulders and stepped onto the uneven walkway. Behind her, she could hear Patricia grumbling as she followed.

Elizabeth walked boldly up onto the small front porch and paused before the large, dark door. The house was even creepier close up. Paint was peeling off the door frame, and the boards below her feet felt warped. Still, the porch offered some shelter from the wind and the rain.

"I don't think anyone lives here," Patricia said into her ear.

Elizabeth rang the old-fashioned doorbell. She could hear the sound echo through the house, but no one answered. She rang again. Still no answer. Elizabeth went around the side of the house toward a rain-streaked, cracked window. One of the shutters was hanging loose, banging against the side of the house in a forlorn manner. Elizabeth stopped it with her hand as she looked in the window. She could see a large room full of books. It looked like a library. The dust lay heavy over everything.

"A perfect vacation spot," Patricia yelled sarcastically from behind her.

"At least it's out of the wind and the rain," Elizabeth replied seriously. "We can get the blankets from the trunk of the car, and there may be wood inside for a fire. Why don't you stay here while I run back to the car?"

"Oh no," Patricia said. "We'll both go. Maybe someone will have stopped by now, and we won't have to spend the night in this horrid house."

They hurried back to the car. When she saw the massive size of the tree limb lying over the trunk, Elizabeth was glad Patricia had insisted upon coming along. She could never have shifted it alone.

Together they wrestled the limb off the back of the car and pulled the blankets out of the trunk. Thrusting the blankets inside their raincoats to keep them dry, they hurried back to the house. By this time even Patricia was glad to be getting out of the rain.

The front door was unlocked, and it creaked open into a narrow hallway. Elizabeth sneezed as dust tickled her nose. She shivered. The house was chilly, but at least it was dry. The dust was so thick that they left visible footprints on the floor wherever they stepped.

"I am not going upstairs," said Patricia. "Let's just sleep down here."

After eyeing the spooky, dark stairwell, Elizabeth agreed.

The sisters hastily searched the downstairs for some firewood. There were a few small sticks left in the bottom of the wood bin in the huge kitchen, but not enough to start a fire. The wood box in the library was totally empty. After vetoing Patricia's suggestion that they break up some of the chairs to make a fire, Elizabeth decided that they would sleep in the library, which was marginally warmer than the rest of the downstairs. The sisters removed their wet coats and spread them out on a table by the fireplace, hoping they would dry by morning. Then they made a bed out of the blankets and lay down to sleep on the library floor.

Elizabeth wasn't sure what awakened her. Perhaps it was the sudden silence. The storm is over, she thought, opening her eyes.

The room was bright, but the light was strange. The room was filled with the smell of the sea. Elizabeth sat up and gasped. A bedraggled man in rough sailor's clothes was standing next to the fireplace. He was dripping wet and looked as if he were trying to dry himself before the fireplace.

"Who are you?" Elizabeth called out in a strangled whisper. "What are you doing here?"

At the sound of her voice, Patricia sat up. She took one look at the man, gave a small shriek, and buried her head beneath the blanket.

"Is this your house?" Elizabeth continued in a stronger voice. "We're sorry, we needed shelter for the night and we thought no one lived . . ." Her voice trailed off as she belatedly realized that the light was coming not from the window, but from the sailor. He was glowing in the dark.

The blanket beside her was shaking. She could hear Patricia, a confirmed atheist, whispering the Lord's Prayer.

The sailor turned and looked directly at Elizabeth. He frowned as if he did not recognize her and muttered something she could not make out. And then he disappeared.

Elizabeth screamed and joined Patricia under the covers. It's just a dream, she told herself firmly. I was dreaming. The room outside the blankets stayed reassuringly dark. "Just a bad dream," she said aloud. Patricia's only reply was a hastily quoted Psalm 23.

"There are no such things as ghosts," Elizabeth added loudly, to convince herself. She turned over on the hard, dusty floor and firmly closed her eyes.

Beside her Patricia recited every piece of Scripture their mother had ever forced them to learn, from Psalm 100 to the Ten Commandments. Finally, she stopped muttering and went back to sleep.

When Elizabeth awoke, sunlight was streaming in the window. She sat up and tapped Patricia on the shoulder. Patricia shot to her feet with a shriek, got tangled in the blankets, and fell over.

"It's morning. Time to go," said Elizabeth.

"Hallelujah." Untangling herself from the blankets, Patricia practically leapt toward the table by the fireplace to get her coat. And stopped dead.

"Elizabeth," she whispered.

Elizabeth hurried to her sister, who was looking at a patch of water by the fireplace. Beside it, draped across the hearth, was a long piece of seaweed. It had not been there the night before. But when Elizabeth looked around the room, the only footprints she could see in the dust were those of herself and her sister.

"That's enough for me. I'm leaving right now," said Patricia. She grabbed her coat and marched out of the house.

Elizabeth lingered for a moment. The sailor had looked so sad, she thought. She picked up the seaweed and put it into the pocket of her raincoat. Then she touched the puddle of water and smelled her finger. It smelled briny, like water from the ocean. She tasted it. It was salty.

Slowly she followed her sister out of the house and down the road to the car. By the time she arrived, Patricia had flagged down a milk truck. The driver offered them a ride to the nearest town.

After arranging for their car to be towed, Elizabeth asked the owner of the garage about the abandoned house.

"The Allen place?" he replied. "The Allens were an old Cape Cod family. Lived in that house nigh on forever. Old Man Allen and his wife were the last of that family. They only had one son, a boy named Thomas. He was a high-spirited lad and he didn't get along too well with his father. 'Bout twenty years ago Old Man Allen and Thomas had a terrible fight. The old man ordered Thomas out of his house and the boy left. Signed onto a fishing boat and was drowned at sea. His mother died of a broken heart when she got the news. Old Man Allen didn't say much after that, he jest got odder and odder. Finally sold the house and went out west." He paused, frowning at the memory and fiddling nervously with the baseball cap in his hands.

"The family that bought the house from him moved away after only a year," he continued slowly. "They claimed that strange things kept happening at night. The property's changed hands a couple of times, but no one's stayed there long. It's stood empty now for over ten years. You girls didn't happen to see anything while you were there?"

"Absolutely not. I don't believe in ghosts," Patricia told him firmly. Elizabeth put her hand into her coat pocket. I do, she thought.

THE TELLTALE SEAWEED

A few months later Elizabeth attended a local dinner party. Patricia usually accompanied her to such events, but this dinner conflicted with her weekly parish meeting. Patricia's newfound faith on the night they met the ghost had continued long after they left Cape Cod. So Elizabeth found herself partnered with another solo guest at dinner. He was a museum curator, and they realized they had a mutual interest in the paranormal. Finding a sympathetic ear, Elizabeth told him the story of her stay in the haunted house.

The museum curator volunteered to test the seaweed for her if she sent him a sample. She did, and after several days passed Elizabeth finally received a letter. The seaweed, her message said, was a rare type often found on the bodies of the drowned.

2

The Lady in Black

GEORGES ISLAND, MASSACHUSETTS

"Sir!"

The newest recruit at Fort Warren came running along the walkway toward Richard Cassidy. Richard turned impatiently and frowned at the redheaded, freckle-faced recruit. What was his name? Charlie?

"Private," he said gruffly.

The private came to attention and snapped off a salute. "Sir. I found a woman's footprints. In the snow." He hesitated, looking confused and a bit frightened. "But they don't go anywhere. The sentry told me to ask you about it."

Richard Cassidy sighed. "I see you've met the Lady in Black," he said.

"Sir?" asked the private.

"Come, show me the footprints," said Richard Cassidy, "and I'll tell you about our resident ghost."

"Ghost?" The private gulped nervously and glanced around.

"Hasn't anyone told you about the woman in black robes who haunts the fort?" asked Richard.

The private shook his head. "I wouldn't have believed them anyway, sir. There's no such thing as ghosts." He

11

sounded confident enough, but he kept glancing about warily as he led Richard down to the great arched entrance to the fort.

"There." He pointed. In the fresh snow Richard Cassidy could see five footprints. The prints of a woman's shoe, they came out of nowhere and ended abruptly after only a few feet.

"Yes, that must be her. She was a tiny woman," said Richard. He nodded to the sentry on guard by the door and said: "Come, Private. It's time someone told you about the Lady in Black."

Richard Cassidy led the private to the Corridor of Dungeons. He brought chairs into an empty cell, and they sat facing each other as the officer began his story.

"You aren't the first to encounter the Lady in Black. A soldier last year was climbing to the top of the ladder that leads to this corridor. As he approached the top, a woman's voice said: 'Don't come in here!' Gave him quite a start. He hightailed it down that ladder and got the commander, who just laughed and told him not to mind the ghost." Richard Cassidy shook his head reminiscently. "Another poor chap I know was walking his post one night when a pair of cold hands surrounded his neck. He struggled furiously against the strangling grip and finally broke free. He turned to confront his attacker and saw the Lady in Black. Unfortunately the commander did not believe his story. The sentry was sentenced to thirty days' solitary confinement for leaving his post."

"Who is this ghost?" asked the private curiously.

"The Lady in Black came originally from the South," Richard Cassidy said, settling back comfortably in his chair. "Her name was Melanie and she was married to a Confederate lieutenant in the Southern army—Samuel Lanier—just a few weeks before he and many others were captured by Burnside at Roanoke Island.

"Sam Lanier was shipped up here to Fort Warren and was incarcerated right here in the Corridor of Dungeons. Somehow, God knows how, he managed to get a message to his wife by the Underground Railroad. The message contained directions on where he was imprisoned and how she could reach him. Being madly in love with her lieutenant, Melanie took passage on a ship and sailed north to Hull."

"What did she do then?" asked the private.

"At that time there was a Confederate sympathizer living in Hull," Richard Cassidy replied. "As soon as she landed, Melanie Lanier located his house. He gave her a pepperbox pistol and a Union soldier's uniform to wear. On a moonless night, she rowed to Georges Island and landed on the beach."

"Plucky woman," said the private admiringly. "You don't meet many girls like that now."

Richard frowned at him. "May I continue?" he asked sarcastically.

"Sorry, sir."

Richard Cassidy continued. "Melanie slipped past the sentries under the cover of the darkness. She gave a prearranged signal and waited tensely for a response. After a few moments she was pulled up to the carronade embrasure and hauled through a musket loop.

"After a tender reunion with her husband, Melanie was told about a tunnel the prisoners were digging under the parade grounds. They were planning to enter the armory and take over the fort. Unfortunately, the prisoners miscalculated. The tunnel came too close to the Union soldiers who were stationed near the wall, and that very night they heard the sounds of digging. The plan was discovered, and Colonel Dimmick immediately came to the Corridor of Dungeons.

"When the colonel cornered Samuel and Melanie Lanier in the cell, she pulled out her pistol and attempted to fire at him. Unfortunately, the pistol exploded. A piece of metal pierced her husband's brain, killing him instantly."

"Oh no," said the private.

"It gets worse," said Richard. "Colonel Dimmick had no choice but to sentence Melanie to hang as a Southern spy. Being a kind man, he gave the woman one last request. Plucky to the end, Melanie wished to be hanged in women's clothing. Soldiers were sent to scour the fort for some women's clothing. The best they could find were some black monk's robes worn by one of the men during an entertainment. Dressed all in black, Melanie Lanier was hanged to death as a Southern spy."

"And now she haunts the fort," said the private.

"Yes, she does," said the officer. "Soldiers have reported seeing a spirit dressed in black walking the parapets and ramparts at night. Several men have shot at her ghost while on sentry duty. The bullets pass right through her. There used to be a regular poker game in the ordnance room, but the Lady in Black kept rolling a stone across the length of the storeroom each time they played. It made the men so nervous they finally chose another part of the island on which to play."

"Thank you, sir, for telling me about the ghost," the private said.

"Just don't desert your post if she comes walking toward you late one night," said Richard, rising from his chair.

THE LADY IN BLACK

"No, sir." The private hurried out of the cell and then turned back toward Richard Cassidy. "Sir, do you really believe in ghosts?" he asked.

"Son," the man replied, "remember I told you about the chap who got thirty days' solitary confinement for being strangled?"

"Yes, sir."

"That man was me," said Richard Cassidy.

3

The Blue Rock

MARTHA'S VINEYARD, MASSACHUSETTS

The story was whispered from person to person, from generation to generation. It was told furtively, in lowered voices. Buried treasure. Near the blue rock. When pressed for details, the person might be willing to tell the whole story.

A long time ago, an unknown ship dropped anchor in the surf near Wasque Bluff, and a small boat carrying a mysterious figure, six sailors, and a large box landed on the beach. The sailors dug a deep hole inland near the blue rock, and the box was lowered into it. As the sailors stepped back, their leader, with an invocation to the father of pirates, threw a small green package onto the box. With a huge crash and a flash of blinding green light, the hole disappeared! The silent group walked back to the boat, leaving behind scorched, blackened earth and one very frightened observer, hidden in the grass.

At this point most people refused to continue the story, although it is common knowledge among the island's inhabitants that the treasure had not been recovered. When pressed, people who sought the treasure would grow pale and allude to dim, threatening figures, a bright green flash, and holes that disappeared without a trace. It was thought best to stop questioning them at this point to give the poor folks time to recover.

After hearing several whispered versions of the story, two adventurers decided to have a go at the treasure. They agreed to meet at the rock at midnight. The first chap arrived a little early. Tired out from his long walk, he leaned against the large stone and closed his eyes.

A sound from the waters of nearby Cape Poge jerked him awake. It was a dark night, with only a sliver of a moon to give light. Turning around, the treasure hunter could just make out the lines of a very large ship, sails set, coming in fast toward shore. There was no one moving on deck, and no one stood at the wheel. Yet the ship dodged the shoals and shallows as expertly as any fisherman on the island. Just when it seemed she would come to ruin and run aground, every sail dropped instantly and the ship drifted gently forward until her keel lightly touched the sandy shore.

The treasure hunter stared at the large, silent ship, shivering slightly, though he wasn't sure why. A plank suddenly ran out from the ship under its own power, for still there was no one to be seen. And then, with a horrible shout, the hatch crashed open and a group of glowing skeletons came swarming out onto the deck. They were a merry crew, joking and laughing as they handed around spades and shovels. Then they came filing down the plank, carrying a dead body.

The skeletons came right toward the rock. They stopped a few yards from the treasure hunter and started to dig. The earth seemed to help them, for almost instantly there was a deep hole, and the spades rang as they hit metal. The treasure hunter caught a glimpse of a large box filled with gold and silver, onto which the corpse was tumbled. As the hole was being refilled, one of the skeletons looked toward the blue rock and stopped shoveling. The others immediately spotted the intruder and came for him.

The treasure hunter was so stiff with fear that he couldn't run. The skeletons swarmed around him like bees and lifted him up, bearing him back toward the hole. Realizing at the last moment that they intended to bury him alive with the corpse, the treasure hunter gave an almighty screech that frightened even these terrible ghosts. They dropped him, and his head fell with a bang against a rock.

For a moment he saw stars. But fear overcame dizziness. He pushed himself up as quickly as his whirling head would allow, to find that the phantoms were gone. He was alone with the blue rock and the waves. No skeletons, no ship, no corpse, not even any treasure could be seen in the dim light of the moon. He could not even tell where they had dug the hole.

Oddly enough, this scared the treasure hunter even worse than the phantoms. Giving another of those terrible shrieks, he hightailed it for home. When his friend arrived at the blue rock a little after midnight, all was dark and lonely.

Quizzed the next day about his defection, the treasure hunter reluctantly told his friend the story. His unfeeling friend clapped him on the shoulder and said: "Better you than me." But somehow, neither of them ever went back for the treasure.

A few years later a new whisper circulated the island. A mysterious stranger was said to have appeared to claim the box.

THE BLUE ROCK

The prints he left in the sand had strange cleft marks in the heel. The stranger then sailed away on a strange ship that had been hovering on the edge of the horizon for several days.

Perhaps the story was true, for there were no more mysterious happenings at the blue rock, and anyone who digs there now is left undisturbed.

4

The Voyage of the Palatine

BLOCK ISLAND, RHODE ISLAND

The *Palatine* gleamed in the sunlight as she set off for the American colonies with a full crew, a long list of German passengers, and a hull crammed with supplies to last through the winter of 1750–51. Certainly there was no indication on that crystal-clear morning of the destiny fate had in store for the ship.

It was not until after the first of the winter storms had blown the ship off course that the passengers began to hear several of the more militant members of the crew muttering against the captain. He was working them too hard, they said. They were not being paid enough money. The passengers were too demanding. The captain had more respect for the passengers than for his own crew.

As storm after storm tore into the *Palatine*, the mutters grew louder and seemed to encompass the whole crew. Black looks followed the passengers wherever they went. Mothers began confining their children to the passenger areas of the ship, fearing trouble.

And trouble came. At the height of a terrible storm, the passengers awoke to loud stomping and yelling above their heads. The crew was attacking the captain in his cabin.

A few of the bravest men made their way up to the storm-lashed deck. The sight that met their eyes was horrific. The crew were keelhauling the captain. They tied his body to the bow of the ship, prepared to leave him there until he drowned. A workman named Gunter gave a mighty shout and tried to rescue the captain. One of the sailors, a shaggy black-bearded man, pulled out a pistol and shot Gunter in the chest. He sank to his knees and then fell onto the deck. Another man tried to rush the mutineers when he realized Gunter was dead, and he, too, was shot.

Picking up Gunter's body and using it as a ram, two of the other mutineers pushed the man back down into the hold. Several crewmen were sent with guns to round up the other passengers, who were thrust into four small rooms. Gunter's wife gave a terrible cry when she saw her dead husband. The black-bearded mutineer laughed, threw the body into the room at her feet, and then barricaded the door. Two men rushed the door, but the mutineers fired a few rounds straight through the wood, wounding one of the men. The passengers rebelled no more.

During the days that followed, the sailors forced the passengers to pay exorbitant prices for a bit of bread and some water to drink. They jeered at the passengers' pleas for mercy, ignoring the cries of the children and the men's angry threats. One morning when the pitifully small rations for the day were brought to the passengers, Gunter's widow threw herself through the door, screaming her rage and rebellion as she beat the sailors with her fists. The sailors laughed and took her away with them—to what end the others did not like to think.

Terrified, the passengers could do nothing but ride out the next series of storms sent by the devils that rule the Atlantic in winter. The *Palatine* came to ruin just off Block Island on a dark, stormy night. The mutineers plundered the ship, ran her aground on the rocks near the shore, and set fire to her.

Realizing their intentions, Gunter's widow, who had been driven mad by her cruel treatment, broke the bonds that held her and raced through the flames to the side of the ship, determined to make the mutineers die with her. But one of the sailors drew his cutlass and cut off her hands as she clung to the gunwale of the last boat to leave the ship. She fell back into the flames, as her murderers lowered the boat onto the ocean and rowed away.

Belowdecks, the strange listing of the ship alarmed the passengers. When they smelled the smoke, the men broke down the doors, fearing fire more than the threat of the mutineers. They gathered the women and children as best they could, but a few of the compartments had struck rock and the prisoners inside were drowned. With the water creeping closer every moment, the men herded the women and children up to the deck. They were met with sheets of fire everywhere they turned—blocking all means of escape.

"I will climb the rigging and try to jump over the side of the boat into the sea," the man leading the way said loudly. The terrified passengers turned hopefully at the sound of his voice. "The shore cannot be too far. I will go for help. Meanwhile, stay away from the fire. Use the water in the hold to douse as many of the flames as you can."

"I will go with you," volunteered another young man.

"And I," said a third.

The three men climbed up the nearest rigging, going as high as they could in order to jump over the fire. But a strong

THE VOYAGE OF THE *PALATINE*

gust of wind fanned the flames nearest the rigging, and the sails began to burn. The passengers watched in horror as the flames swiftly overtook the men. The leader, on fire from head to foot, lost his grip and plummeted to the rocks below, followed swiftly by the two other volunteers.

The rest of the passengers panicked. Some hurried below, where they blockaded themselves against the flames. Others plunged through the flames and leapt into the sea. On shore, the islanders were gathering to render what aid they could to the stricken ship and her passengers. But by sunrise the *Palatine* had burned and slipped beneath the waves. There were only a few survivors.

Every winter since then, just before a storm, the *Palatine* reappears off the shore and is wrecked and burned before the eyes of any who watch for her.

5

The Ghost of Elvira Blood

BLACK ROCK HARBOR, CONNECTICUT

Well, if you're lookin' for ghosts, you won't find a feistier one than Mrs. Sam Blood who haunts the tavern over yonder. You never heard the story? Well, set you down and I'll tell you all about it.

Now, ol' Sam Blood was a big, brawny sea captain who ran a large brig outta Black Rock Harbor that made short trips to Atlantic seaports. When he was home between trips, he visited the tavern every night, him being a member of the Mariner's Club that liked to dine there. The Mariner's Club was full of old salts who gathered in the tavern whenever they were ashore, trading tall tales, planning new ventures, drinking deeply, and feasting merrily at that old oaken table in the back room upstairs.

Sam Blood had married young and fathered a large number of untidy children. His wife was a tall, gaunt woman of a sickly disposition and a tendency to whine over ol' Sam's shortcomings, which he had in abundance. His mother, an old battle-ax with a tendency to rule the roost, also lived on the old farm where Sam kept his family in isolation a few miles outside town.

Well, ol' Sam's boozing and carousing had been goin' on for several years when Elvira Blood finally got fed up with making do on the little money that was left after Sam attended a "meeting" of the Mariner's Club. Now, Elvira mighta been sickly, but deep down she had good ol' New England blood in her veins and was made of sterner material than anyone 'round here suspected. She decided that the Mariner's Club, and Sam in particular, needed a lesson.

Hearing 'bout a particularly big feast prepared for the club one winter's night, Elvira Blood raided her husband's closet and dressed up in Sam's togs. She crept up to the well-lit tavern, where she could hear the old salts in the Mariner's Club, her husband the loudest of the bunch, whooping it up in the taproom. A servant girl was running up and down the back staircase to the second-floor dining room with steaming dishes of hot food. When the girl finished her tasks and departed to the taproom to announce dinner, Elvira Blood slid through the door and ran up the stairs.

A magnificent feast was spread on the large round table at the center of the room. Elvira drew in a breath of rage at the sight. There were roasts and boiled meats, pies and puddings, breads, sweets, and all sorts of bottles and decanters of wine. All Elvira could afford to serve her children that night was a thin soup made mostly of leeks and carrots, while her rotten husband Sam had been downstairs preparing for a night of feasting.

Elvira snatched a corner of the white tablecloth and yanked it off the table with a scream of rage. The dishes came crashin' to the floor, the bottles and decanters spillin' their contents and the roasts, pies, puddings, and breads tangling into a big, ruined heap half on the table and half on the floor. Grinning evilly, Elvira knocked the table completely on its side, spillin' the rest of its contents. Then she ran down the back staircase and out the kitchen door.

THE GHOST OF ELVIRA BLOOD

Down in the taproom the sound of the crashin' dishes had silenced the noise. The landlord and his guests leapt to their feet and rushed upstairs. They paused in the doorway to the dining room, starin' in amazement at the mess. Then one of the captains ran to the window. He saw in the moonlight a thin figure in nautical garb fleeing across the snowy field away from the inn.

"There he goes!" he shouted. The men gave pursuit, and the swiftest of them soon overtook Elvira and swung her 'round with oaths and blows. Sam's cap fell off her head, and the members of the Mariner's Club grew suddenly silent as they recognized her. Sam turned crimson. "I'll settle for this dinner," he said darkly.

"You'll settle for more than that, Sam Blood," said Elvira angrily. "Feastin' with these sinners while your children starve."

Furious and embarrassed, Sam hustled his wife home before she could say anything more. But the damage was done. By midday all the men and women in town had heard the story, and their sympathy was for the "plucky" Mrs. Blood rather than for her husband. Everyone was talking about how Elvira had shamed the "sinners" with her act of destruction.

By the end of the month, all the wives in town had decided that poor, overworked Mrs. Blood needed a change of scene. Universal opinion bein' against him, Sam Blood had no choice but to take Elvira with him on his next voyage—that being the only option he could afford after payin' for the ruined dinner.

Elvira was none too pleased with the arrangement. She was the only woman on a ship full of rough sailors, and she was forced to travel in discomfort from port to port. By the time the ship reached Savannah, she had returned to her sickly, whining ways.

Sam Blood, aware that he would be run out of town if he brought his wife home in her current condition, decided to sail on to South America, hopin' that the tropical air might improve Elvira's health and disposition. His regular crew, not caring to continue on another long trip with the weepy Elvira, shipped back to Boston while Sam and Elvira traveled onward with a hired crew.

When Sam Blood returned home, he was a widower. Somberly, he told the townsfolk that Elvira had passed to her reward on the seas just off Jamaica. He put on mourning for his dead wife and walked around with a sober countenance for several months. But he was quickly back to his old ways, spendin' most of his time and money at the tavern among the members of the Mariner's Club while his old mother took care of the children. Elvira Blood was forgotten.

A year to the day after the spoiled feast, the old salts were once again in the tavern taproom waitin' to dine in the upstairs room. Ol' Sam, suitably somber, was among the guests who lingered at the bar as the rest made their way to the staircase. The landlord was standing at the top of the stairs, callin' the mariners to dinner, when a horrible crashing and banging sound came from the dining room. Everyone ran to the door as they had done the year before. The table was lying on its side with the dishes, roasts, pies, puddings, and decanters spilled out upon the floor. Sam Blood turned purple, unpleasantly reminded of the mortifying events of the previous year.

A thorough search was made, but no culprit was found. The landlord finally blamed a discharged servant, and the disgruntled members of the Mariner's Club went home to eat. The next week a second feast was laid on that table. As the landlord carried a roast upstairs to the room, tremendous crashing and banging sounds echoed again through the tavern. The Mariner's Club found the table tipped on its side and the dinner ruined. This time they all looked at Sam Blood. The widower stood like a stone; his face was calm, but his large, tattooed hands were shakin'.

After a third and a fourth incident, Sam Blood was barred from the Mariner's Club, and the landlord wouldn't let him in the tavern for a drink. More meals were laid on that table, but no one ever got to eat them. As soon as the room was empty, the table was overturned, and the dishes smashed. The landlord even had the table legs nailed to the floor, to no avail. He tried settin' watchers, but something always distracted them at the last moment and over the table would go, nails and all.

Sam Blood was blamed for the decay and dissolution of the once popular Mariner's Club in this town. The heart went right out of the club when they finally realized they could never dine again in the upstairs room. When other mariners' events were staged in other communities, Sam Blood was never invited. No one wanted to associate with a man who'd left shore with a wife and come home with a ghost.

So Elvira had her way after all. Sam Blood's carousin' days were over. No one but his family would associate with him, and he died a lonely man. Sam Blood is long gone now and buried up on the hill. But Elvira Blood still upsets that dang-blasted table in the tavern whenever anyone is foolish enough to leave food there.

6

The Watcher of the Isles of Shoals

STAR ISLAND, NEW HAMPSHIRE, AND APPLEDORE, MAINE

His health was failing that summer of 1826. He felt in his bones that he would not live much longer. His family, less resigned to fate than he, endeavored to bring him back to health by sending him to stay with a fisherman and his family on Star Island, which was part of the Isles of Shoals.

Summer slowly turned to autumn, and the solitude of the islands brought some solace to him. Watching the sun rise over the ocean, hearing the endless sound of the waves and the calling of birds, helped reconcile him to the immortality of the soul. It was autumn, and the mornings were remote and still. Strength slowly returned to his body, and he began to take short walks and even to sail a small boat around the islands.

One afternoon he rowed over to the island of Appledore for a stroll. The island was uninhabited and had been so ever since Maine taxes were assessed for the island township in the 1680s. The independent Shoalers, forty families strong, had decided they would rather live in New Hampshire than pay Maine taxes, so they had dismantled their homes and moved to Star Island. He chuckled to himself at the thought.

His wanderings took him out onto a long, low point backed by cliffs. He faced east, gazing across the sea. Suddenly he became aware of a woman standing but a few feet away. He had no notion from whence she came. He had heard no footsteps, seen no movement. She wore a dark cape, and her fair hair spilled over her shoulders. Her face was beautiful, but wan, and her blue eyes were fixed on the distance.

She must, he decided, be waiting for a fishing boat. Or perhaps she had a tryst here with a lover. He stood in silence, not wishing to disturb her reverie. At length, when no boat appeared in the distance, he said: "Do you see anything of him?"

She fixed melancholy blue eyes upon him and said: "He will come again." She turned away and walked out of sight around a jutting rock. Amazed, he took a few steps after her. But when he reached the rock, she had disappeared. His skin prickled with superstitious fear, for he could see no place where she could have hidden, nor any reason for her to do so. He suddenly wished himself safe in his quarters on Star Island and beat a hasty retreat to his boat.

Back in his room, he thought perhaps the woman had been a dream, or an illusion brought about by his illness. She haunted his thoughts. The rest of the day, he gazed anxiously into the face of each of the women he saw on Star Island, hoping to see the woman he had met on Appledore. But there was none who resembled her. And when he described her to his hostess, she said she had never heard of her.

The next day the wind blew up a gale. He knew he should not go out in such weather, but he was haunted by the memory of the disappearing woman and was driven to return to Appledore to verify or deny her existence. Ignoring the warning of the fisherman, he sailed his small boat across the furious waves and found shelter in a cove on the leeward side of the island. He made his way to the point, but found it buried under a rolling sea. As he stood in the fierce wind, he heard a voice call over the waves: "He will come again." And then, as close as a breath, a low laugh sounded beside him. He whirled in terror, but there was no one there.

Obsessed with a desire to meet the woman again, he began visiting the island every day. As he stood on the point, often the golden-haired woman stood with him. His first terror gone, he noticed details about her now. The shells were not crushed beneath her feet. The wind never ruffled her hair. Her garments never rustled as she moved. And her attitude was one of deep stillness. Always, whether she spoke or stood in silence, he could sense her words: "He will come again."

He was shaky, jittery at all times now. The fisherman and his family were worried by his sudden nervous condition. But he could not seem to refrain from visiting the island with its ghost.

Then one evening as he stood on the western shore of Appledore, gazing at the sunset, the woman appeared beside him. As they watched the fishing boats unfurl their white sails and depart for the night's fishing from the cove of Star Island, he turned to look at his companion. Just for a moment, in the light of sunset, the blue eyes softened and he could see the warmth and humanity that she had once possessed. The sight alarmed him as her presence never had. She had once been as human as he. What tragedy had tied her to this island, never to rest? The terror, held in check for many days, overwhelmed him and he ran away, vowing never to come again to Appledore or look upon its ghost.

THE WATCHER OF THE ISLES OF SHOALS

Unbeknownst to him, the old fisherman, concerned for his health, had delayed his fishing that night in order to discover where his guest kept going. Upon his return from Appledore, the fisherman met him on the dock on Star Island. They walked together for a few moments in silence. Then the fisherman quietly told him the story of the Watcher.

Captain Teach, better known as Blackbeard, had once terrorized these waters. One of his comrades, a pirate called Captain Scot, had brought this fair lady to the Isles of Shoals. It was said that immense treasure had been buried by Blackbeard on Lunging, but Scot had buried his treasure separately and had made his lover swear that she would guard the treasure from all comers until he returned, be it until the Day of Judgment. Departing on a voyage to plunder, slash, and slay, Captain Scot was accidentally killed when a powder magazine blew up, leaving the woman alone to guard his treasure until the end of time.

"She is still there," said the fisherman. "Watching."

They both looked across the water at Appledore. The ghost's words rang once more through the man's mind: "He will come again." He wondered if she knew that her pirate lover was lost to her forever. He sighed, and his companion clapped a hand on his arm.

"Let's go home," said the fisherman. The man nodded. They turned away from the ghost of the past and headed for the warmth and light of home.

7

The Ghosts of Georges Bank

GLOUCESTER, MASSACHUSETTS

The *Charles Haskell* was a beautiful schooner, built in 1869 for a sea captain who fished Georges Bank for a living. But on the night she was completed, a workman making one last inspection slipped on the forecastle companion. He was found dead of a broken neck the next morning at the bottom of the companion ladder. Such an omen could not be ignored, the captain felt, and he refused to complete his purchase of the ship. Winter-fishing Georges Bank was difficult enough without beginning the venture with an ill-fated sign.

Georges Bank often saw tragedy, especially during winter gales when cables parted and ships were set adrift to almost certain collision with other crafts fishing the area. A year passed, and finally another Gloucester captain did take the *Haskell* to sea. The crew were handlining for cod some forty miles west of Georges North Shoal. The luck was in, and the men were fishing fast.

"We've got a bit o' wind coming tonight, gentlemen, yes sir," commented Joe Enos, the only Portuguese sailor on board the *Haskell*. Joe normally didn't have much to say for himself, but he was a grand fisherman, and the crew knew that when he spoke they'd better listen up. If Joe thought a "bit o' wind" was coming, then chances were good that he was right.

"What makes you say so?" asked George Scott.

"See the way the fish are takin' the hook? I've never seen 'em bite like this unless a bit o' wind were coming by and by," said Joe. "Look around. It's the same everywhere."

George looked around. Within five or six miles of the *Haskell*, about a hundred ships were pulling in cod as fast as they could get their lines in the water. It was quite a sight.

"A bit o' wind," George said uneasily, tossing out his lead.

Around noon the wind shifted into the east-northeast and began rising steadily. By three o'clock Captain Curtis had ordered the crew to haul in their lines. The men gave the *Haskell* eighty more fathoms on the cable. Then they prepared a balanced-reefed mainsail in case of storm and prepared it for quick hoisting should they go adrift.

By nine o'clock Joe's "bit o' wind" was a full-fledged hurricane. There were 290 vessels out on Georges Bank that night, with the deadly North Shoal under the lee of the fleet. Aboard the *Haskell* all hands were on the heaving deck. Captain Curtis himself was stationed beside the cable, holding an ax. Through the sleet, the crew could see the lights of unlucky vessels passing them in a ghastly parade, having broken adrift in the storm.

The *Haskell* was dragging anchor, but before she slipped far the anchor caught on something and the ship stopped short. She hung above the bank, buffeted relentlessly by the huge waves, when the men at the forward lookout gave a shout: "Light!"

A light was riding directly over the schooner's bowsprit. Captain Curtis cut the line, and the *Haskell* catapulted away from its mooring. The strange vessel swept by.

"Up the foresail," shouted the captain. "Joe, keep her due west!"

Joe Enos nodded. The captain wanted to get them leeward of the fleet and beyond the North Shoal. If the *Haskell* stayed here, there was precious little choice between collision and going aground. Joe kept her due west.

They ran westward for half an hour before they raised another light just off the bow.

"Hard up the helm," called Curtis, thinking the vessel was riding anchor.

But the other ship was also adrift. She, too, hove up hard at the sight of the *Haskell*. From the crest of a wave, the *Haskell* crashed into the other ship, cutting her down just aft of the port rigging. The strange vessel was split nearly to the mainmast. For a frozen moment, the crews of both ships could see each other clearly. They were so close that one or two of the stranger's crewmen could have jumped aboard the *Haskell*. But no one moved. A moment later the vessel, with her crew, vanished beneath the waves.

The main boom and rigging on the starboard side of the *Haskell* had been carried away in the crash. The bowsprit had cracked and bent. It was thudding ominously against the bow. The men rushed to cut it free and then secured the mast as best they could.

As soon as the initial wreckage was cleared, Joe Enos went below to check for damage. The *Haskell* would be taking on water by now; no ship stayed afloat after a collision. He found George down in the forecastle, almost hysterical with relief.

"She's dry, Joe. She's dry!" George screamed and then laughed frantically. "There ain't a drop in her."

"Now, George," Joe said, alarmed by the man's behavior. This was no time for George to lose his head. Joe took up the trap in the floor and looked in. There was no water underneath. Not a drop.

"*Deos!*" Joe said.

He ran to tell the captain. Curtis immediately instructed his men to try the pump. They quickly realized that the *Charles Haskell* was dry. The men's relief was palpable. Suddenly everyone believed that they would weather this storm and make it home.

But Joe turned to the captain and said: "Those poor sailors, Captain. I could see their faces—one, two men clear as day. Such a look on their faces."

Captain Curtis gave a grim nod and looked into the sleet-spattered waves. He asked: "Did you see what vessel she was?"

"No, Captain. I will ask the others." But no one knew.

When the *Haskell* limped home to Gloucester, they learned that nine ships had gone down on the bank that night. All but three schooners were accounted for; of those remaining, the *A. E. Price* and *Martha Porter* were out of Gloucester, and the *Andrew Johnson* was out of Salem. Captain Curtis knew the skippers of all three, but supposed he would never know which the *Haskell* had rammed in the storm.

The *Haskell* was run up on the flats for repair and refitting. While she was there, many hundreds came to look at this ship that had survived a collision on the bank. No one had ever heard of such a thing in all the history of Georges. But an old fisherman told Captain Curtis that he should find another ship. After sending ten men to the bottom of Georges Bank, the *Haskell* would bring him bad luck.

Captain Curtis turned pale and shouted at the old fellow: "We ain't got no blood on our hands!"

Despite the captain's reassurances, two of his men refused to ship out on the *Haskell* again; Captain Curtis had to find replacements. But the rest of the crew stuck by him. And glad they were of it, for on the next trip out, Georges gave them some beautiful fishing.

On their sixth day at sea, Joe Enos and Harry Richardson had the midnight watch. Joe was nodding over the wheel, trying to stay awake, when Harry poked him in the ribs. Joe started awake, saying: "Whatcha doing that for, Harry?"

Joe blinked blearily at his watchmate. Harry was pale and shaking. Unable to say a word, he pointed forward. Joe stared over the wheel. In the starlight he could make out a small group of men up in the bow.

"What they doin' up at this hour? You'd think they'd want a bit o' shut-eye," said Joe, shaking his head.

"Joe, look at 'em again," Harry gasped. "They ain't our boys!"

Joe frowned at Harry and took a few steps forward. Then he stopped. The group was growing. Before his eyes, he could see a man climbing over the rail on the starboard side. And then another. They were coming out of the waters of the bank. Joe carefully withdrew back to where Harry was still standing and shaking. The two men stood silent, watching. Finally Joe whispered: "I'll go get the skipper."

"No you won't! You ain't leavin' me here with them," Harry said fiercely.

"You go then," said Joe.

THE GHOSTS OF GEORGES BANK

But at that moment the men at the bow began stationing themselves at the regular fishing berths along the deck. They baited hooks and heaved lines over the side.

"Joe! Joe, they're fishin'," Harry gasped. The two men watched in amazement. The fishermen ignored them.

"All right," said Joe Enos. "How 'bout this? We stay here until the next watch comes. We don't say nuthin' about this. See what Scotty and O'Neil see."

"All right," said Harry uneasily.

The two men stayed by the wheel box, watching the fishermen casting for and catching invisible fish in the calm starlight. They beat a fast retreat when it came time to call the new watch. Barely had Joe settled down to sleep when he heard a frantic yell from the deck followed by the sound of feet pounding their way to the captain's quarters. A moment later all hands were called on deck.

When Joe went up on deck again, the crew were huddled around the cabin companionway, watching the figures on deck tending their lines and putting their invisible catch into barrels.

"I see 'em. I've got eyes. But we ain't got no blood on our hands. It was an accident, boys." There was mingled anger and appeal in the captain's voice. His eyes were haunted; he kept repeating himself as if pleading for absolution.

"I ain't stayin' here another night," George said. "I'll swim home before I stay here."

"There's a fair wind tonight, Captain," Scotty added.

"We should stay here. I tell you, we ain't got blood on our hands," shouted the captain. Then he glanced at the silent fishermen and everyone lowered their voices. Not, Joe Enos noticed, that the men fishing the lines took any notice of them.

They smiled and spoke silently to each other as they worked, but did not seem to see the real crew.

The argument raged for several more minutes before the captain, alone in his stand, finally gave in.

"All right, boys," he said wearily. "I still say we ain't got nothin' to fear. But pull in the anchor and we'll go home."

Warily the men went to work. They were reluctant to go near the "extra hands," and this made things difficult, because the silent fishermen were hauling in their lines and preparing to stop for the day. After going through the motions of cleaning up, the men filed to the bow, stepped over the rail, and disappeared into the dark waters of Georges Bank.

Their departure spurred on the crew, and the *Haskell* was soon under way. But the next night, just as the *Haskell* was passing the twin lights of Thacher Island under a good breeze, the phantom crew joined them again. While the visitors fished into the small watches, the *Haskell* came abreast of Eastern Point Light, and the captain took the wheel and steered for Gloucester Harbor.

This caused a stir among the phantom crew. They all turned to look at the captain. Then they went to the bow of the ship. The *Haskell*'s crew were trimming the sails and glancing uneasily at their audience. One of the phantoms came aft as far as the forerigging and shook his head at the captain. The *Haskell* was making fast for Gloucester Harbor, and the captain held to his course. So the phantom mounted the rail, beckoned to his crewmates, and disappeared over the side. The others followed him.

Joe Enos gazed after them, and then called: "Captain! Captain, they're marchin' across the water. They're headin' toward Salem."

Safely moored again in Gloucester Harbor, the crew departed the *Haskell*, never to board her again. From that moment the *Haskell* was taboo in Gloucester. Not for love or money could Captain Curtis get anyone to sail her. Only Joe Enos was willing to try again.

"Because I understand now, Captain," he said to Curtis. "Them was the crew of the *Andrew Jackson*, sir. After we fish Georges the next time, we sail first to Salem. We take them home. Then everything will be right with the *Haskell*."

But the Captain did not believe him.

Unable to get a crew, the *Haskell* lay for months in Gloucester Harbor. Finally she was sold to a group in Nova Scotia. She never sailed Georges Bank again.

8

Ocean-born Mary

HENNIKER, NEW HAMPSHIRE

"Have you ever seen her?" I asked an old Henniker man casually as I stood looking at Ocean-born Mary's tombstone behind the town hall. I was spending my vacation in Henniker that year because I was intrigued by the story of the town's red-haired ghost. Since I too was tall, red-haired, and named Mary, I felt a certain kinship with the ghost.

"Seen who?" he asked testily, glancing at me suspiciously from his pious stance in front of a nearby tombstone.

"Ocean-born Mary," I said. "Have you ever seen her ghost over at the house? Or here? Mr. Roy said she rises from this grave and travels in a carriage drawn by four horses to her old home."

"Did Mr. Roy also try to rent you a shovel to dig for treasure in the orchard?" the old man asked sarcastically. "Or didn't he tell you about the time Mary saw her pirate and his minion carrying a large chest out to the orchard?"

"Perhaps he did offer me a shovel," I said with dignity. "But everyone knows that the pirate and his treasure are buried under the hearthstone of the house he built for Mary."

"Oh, everyone knows, do they?"

"Common knowledge," I said in a toplofty manner. This small, bent old man was beginning to irritate me. I had taken precious time away from my job to visit the house and town haunted by Ocean-born Mary, and I didn't like the way he seemed to regard my trip as a joke.

I don't normally go ghost hunting, but the story of Ocean-born Mary had intrigued me at once. Her parents, Elizabeth and James Wilson, were immigrants from Londonderry, Ireland. In 1720 they set sail for America. They had been granted some land in Londonderry, New Hampshire, and were hoping to start a new life there.

As they neared Boston, Elizabeth went into labor and gave birth to a daughter. While she was giving birth, a strange vessel accosted the ship. They were fired upon and forced to heave to. Their ship was boarded by a band of swarthy pirates. Their leader, a surprisingly young man not yet twenty years of age, was dark, handsome, and ruthless. He was called Don Pedro, and his English was flawless as he ordered all the captives killed.

At this fatal juncture, the cries of a newborn baby could be heard from down in the hold. Startled, Don Pedro ordered the captain to take him to the child. After gazing for a long time at the tiny girl, Don Pedro said to Elizabeth: "If you name this child after my mother—Mary—I will spare the lives of everyone on this ship." Frightened by the fierce pirate, Elizabeth hastily agreed.

Don Pedro sent one of his men back to the pirate ship. When the man returned, he was carrying an armload of gifts. Don Pedro presented these to Elizabeth. Fingering a green brocaded silk with an odd look of tenderness on his ruthless face, he said: "This is for my Mary's wedding dress." Then he and his men returned to their ship and departed.

OCEAN-BORN MARY

Soon after their ship landed safely in Boston, James Wilson died. His widow and daughter went to Londonderry to claim the land in his name. Ocean-born Mary grew into a tall, beautiful red-haired woman. In 1742, wearing a green brocade gown made from the silk given to her by Don Pedro, Mary was married to James Wallace. They had five children, four sons and a daughter. Sadly, after the birth of his fourth son, James Wallace died.

Around that time Don Pedro, having retired from the sea, decided to build a home in New Hampshire. Having never forgotten his little Ocean-born Mary, he began seeking to discover what became of her. Finding her a widow in Londonderry, he married her and brought her and her children to live in his grand mansion in Henniker. He gifted Mary with a stately coach and four, in which Mary would often be seen riding around the countryside. One by one her sons grew up, married, and settled down near Mary.

One day, coming in from an errand to town, Mary saw Don Pedro and one of his retired pirates carrying a large black trunk to the orchard in back. She heard the sounds of digging, and then silence. Don Pedro came back to the house alone, and they never spoke of the matter. But later he told Mary that when he died, she should bury him and the treasure under the hearthstone. A year passed, and Mary came home one evening to an empty house. She started searching for her husband and found Don Pedro in the orchard, stabbed to death with a cutlass. Mary buried Don Pedro with his treasure under the hearthstone, and there they lie to this day.

After her death in 1814, Mary's ghost began to haunt the house. People would see a tall, beautiful red-haired woman come walking down the long staircase. Sometimes she could be seen standing beside an upper window, or throwing something down the well. Mr. Roy had witnessed Mary driving in her coach and four up to the front door of the house. Just that morning I myself had seen her rocking chair begin to move in greeting as I came into the room.

"Common knowledge," chuckled the bent old man, breaking into my thoughts. "Ha! I suppose you were also taken in by that fake rocking chair old Roy has set up. He jiggles a loose floorboard with his foot just as some fool comes through the door and then says Mary set the rocking chair moving to greet her guest."

I flushed a bright red. "So you're saying there is no ghost?"

"I never said there wasn't a ghost," said the old man, fixing bright blue eyes on me. "But Mary never lived in that 'Ocean-born Mary' house. No, miss, that house was built by her son Robert, and Mary never lived with Robert. Mary lived about half a mile away, with her son William. Moved in with William when she was seventy-eight years old. William's house was the one that Mary haunted; she often stood at the windows, walked down the staircase, threw something in the well. William's house is gone now. The town made it into a poorhouse in 1844, and later it was destroyed by vandals."

But it wasn't the change in the location of the haunted house that concerned me.

"Mary moved to Henniker when she was seventy-eight years old?" I asked, stunned by this revelation. "You mean she never married Don Pedro?"

Finding out the Ocean-born Mary house was a fake was bad enough. But I had loved Mary's story best for its romance—the young pirate seeking out the child he had named, falling in love with her, taking her to live with him in his grand mansion.

"Now, young lady, I never said that either," the old man replied.

"But you said she lived with her son William. That the Ocean-born Mary house never belonged to Don Pedro. That Mary was *seventy-eight years old* when she came to Henniker."

I sounded like a whiny child, but I couldn't help it. I was completely crushed by this discovery.

"Look, miss, Don Pedro never lived in Henniker. But my great-granny told me that Mary did marry her pirate, who had taken the name of James Wallace, and she had a very happy life with him until he died in 1791. According to great-granny, the Wallace family never had a son named James until they came to America the year Mary was twelve.

"The Wallaces were a poor family living in Burnt Mills, Scotland. According to great-granny, they talked a lot about going to America, but couldn't afford to buy passage on a ship. Then one night a mysterious stranger visited the Wallaces and offered them money to go to America in exchange for a favor. Sometime during their sea voyage, a man would board their ship, and they were to claim him as their oldest son. The Wallaces agreed to the bargain, as long as their new 'son' was given a Christian name and a new birth date, it being important to Mrs. Wallace that all her children be born in wedlock, so to speak. My great-granny knew Ocean-born Mary, miss. And she said that Mary wore a green brocade gown, the gift of her bridegroom, the day she married James 'Don Pedro' Wallace."

I was intrigued by the old man's story. Had Don Pedro really assumed a new identity under which to woo and win his Ocean-born Mary? I turned back to the man. "How did your great-grandmother learn all this, Mr., Mr. . . ."

"Wallace," he said, giving me an old-fashioned bow. "My name is Charlie Wallace."

I caught my breath in surprise. Could this be a coincidence, or was this man related to Ocean-born Mary?

"You see, miss," he went on with a secretive smile, "my great-granny married a cousin of the Wallace family, and she knew them back when they lived in Burnt Mills. In fact, she stood up with them at their wedding. So she knew that their eldest son was not named James. They had to tell her the truth, miss, what with her being kin and all. Of course, she never said nothing about it while Mary was alive. But she passed the story down to her children, so the truth would not be lost."

"So according to your great-grandmother, Don Pedro became an honest man," I said thoughtfully. "And he settled down in Ocean-born Mary's hometown and waited for her to grow up, so he could woo and marry her."

"They had five children and lived happily together until the end of their days," said old Mr. Wallace. "That's how great-granny always ended the story." He smiled reminiscently. "Well, miss, it has been a pleasure." He tipped his hat and walked away, whistling.

By this time I was completely nonplussed. Who was telling the truth? Was it old Mr. Roy who lived in the haunted Ocean-born Mary house and claimed Mary and Don Pedro had lived there together until Don Pedro died from a cutlass blow to the heart? Or was Charlie Wallace right, and had Mary's son Robert built the Ocean-born Mary house while Mary herself lived in (and haunted) the now-destroyed William Wallace house half a mile away? And as for the story of Don Pedro taking on the identity of James Wallace so he could woo and win Mary . . .

Actually, I liked that story. It might be cockamamie nonsense like the fifty-cent shovels you could rent from Mr. Roy to dig for treasure in the orchard, but it was very romantic, all the same. And there was one point Mr. Roy and Charlie Wallace (who could be in league with each other for all I knew) had agreed upon.

I looked back at the tombstone. "Well, Mary," I said. "I'm not sure anymore what the true story is. But everyone seems to agree that you lived a happy life. And who knows," I added, brightening, "if your son Robert did own the Ocean-born Mary house, then you must have visited it often. So maybe your ghost does pop in from time to time."

I gave the gravestone a pat and followed old Charlie Wallace out of the cemetery.

9

The Wraith in the Storm

BOSTON, MASSACHUSETTS

Tom was just about the most promising child a parent could wish for, at least to hear his parents tell it. They were getting older now, and only had two children left at home—Tom and their youngest, a bright-eyed maiden named Jane.

Tom was an intelligent lad by anyone's reckoning. By the age of twenty-one, he was the first mate on the *Argonaut*. His folks were bursting with pride on the day he set sail for Calcutta out of Boston Harbor. It was the tenth voyage of the *Argonaut*, and Tom's first voyage as first mate. He couldn't wait to kiss his parents good-bye and get on board. They watched him shoulder his pack and stride down the walk, pausing at the gate to rumple the hair of his young sister before striding down the shore road to the harbor.

"Good-bye, Tom. Safe journey," the little girl piped in her high treble, waving her hand until he disappeared from view.

"Safe journey," echoed his mother. She was a little pale, and holding back tears.

Her husband, John, gave her hand a squeeze. "Now, Mandy," he chided. "God'll be with him."

"I know," she replied. "I know. But there's somethin' amiss, Father. I ken feel it."

"What ye feel is chilly. Come in from the cold, Mandy."

"Yes, it's cold. Janie," she called to her youngest, "come in and get yer cloak. The wind is chilly."

"Comin', Mama," Jane said, jumping off the fence and walking obediently up to the house.

The next day a tremendous gale blew in from the east. The storm lasted for days, unrelenting in its fury.

"I knew it. I knew somethin' was amiss," Amanda said over and over to John.

"Hush, Mandy," he said softly. "Don't scare the girl."

Little Jane stood at the window watching the giant waves crashing into the beach, eating away at the sand. "Will Tom be all right, Mama?" she asked gravely.

"We will pray for him, Janie," said her father, unable to lie to the child. She nodded and went back to watching the waves.

They all kept watch, day after day, while the storm raged without ceasing. Hour after hour Amanda knitted socks and rocked back and forth, back and forth in her rocking chair, while her husband read the family Bible. Jane played with her dolls and watched out the window, surprisingly good for such an active little girl. The house shook with gust after gust of wind, the fire hissed and spat in the fireplace as rain made its way down the chimney, and the window grew so rain-streaked that Jane finally abandoned it for some blocks her father had carved for Tom long ago.

On the fourth night of the gale, after Jane was tucked up asleep in her bed, Amanda sat with her knitting in her lap, staring into space. She rocked and rocked as the wind shook the house, and the fire flared up every time a gust of wind came down the chimney. John kept looking at her over his spectacles. She started when their eyes met and tried to knit a few more rows. Finally, she stood up and went to the window, still holding the knitting absently in her hand.

"Tommy, where be ye?" she asked the darkness out the window.

All at once she drew back with a desperate cry. Before her horrified eyes was a shadowy procession, coming up the shore road toward the house. Eight men were carrying a coffin on their shoulders as they moved solemnly through the gale. They paused before the front gate, and the lid of the coffin sprang open to reveal the body of Tom. He lay still in death, a smile of peace on his face.

"My God," Amanda cried, "it's Tom in his coffin!"

The procession turned in at the gate. Amanda stumbled back from the window, dropping her knitting on the floor. "They're bringing him up here, to the house." She covered her face with her hands.

"Mandy," John said in alarm, coming over to the window. He glanced out, but all he saw was darkness. "Mandy, set down. Set down this minute. There's nothin' out there."

"Tom's dead. I know he is. I saw him," Amanda said, raising her face from her hands and looking into her husband's eyes.

"Mandy," said John, "don't you know there ain't no such thing as yer sayin'? There's nobody out there. No man in their right mind would be out there in this storm."

THE WRAITH IN THE STORM

"'Tweren't men out there, John. It were ghosts or maybe spirits," Amanda said. "They came to let me know our boy is dead. So we'd know, John, and not jest think he was missing, like poor old Sarah, still waiting for her missing boy after twenty years."

Amanda was calmer now. She allowed John to push her into the rocker. "Our boy came to say good-bye to us," she told John.

"Don't be making a fool of yerself," John said gruffly, fear clutching at his throat. Mandy sounded so sure.

"You'll see," Amanda said, leaning back in her rocker and closing her eyes. Tears stole out from under her lids and dripped down her cheeks. "You'll see."

The news came a few weeks later. The *Argonaut* was missing. All hands were presumed dead. Tom was never heard from again.

10

Emily's Bridge

No one remembers Emily now, at least not the Emily I knew. Emily lived on the farm next door to mine, just outside of Stowe. She was a few years older than me, but we were friends anyway. We'd walk home from school together when we were younger. Later, when Emily was too old for school, she would come over and show me new ways to do my hair and talk about clothes and beaus. Something I really appreciated, what with me living with three older brothers and having a mother and father in heaven.

'Course, I was always welcomed at Emily's house. They sort of adopted me—"poor parentless Judith from next door." Emily's mother rather pampered me, and her father would give me sweets. Emily's family was well-to-do and they were very proud of their beautiful only daughter. Truthfully, Emily was a bit spoiled and used to having her own way. I was pretty easygoing back then, and I didn't mind when she bossed me around.

Emily had a whole string of suitors coming by regularly, but she didn't seem to have a preference for any of them. Until Peter came to Stowe for an extended visit with his cousins. Peter was the ne'er-do-well son of a miller. He was tall, handsome, and fascinating, and he quickly joined the crowd of young men who waited upon Emily's fancy. Emily's family did not approve of Peter, but they never actually forbade him to see her.

I knew right away that Emily had fallen for him. She turned a pretty pink color when she saw him coming, and she had a way of studying him through her long eyelashes that made me certain her other young suitors were out of the running. Once, on my way home, I spotted them leaning against a tree behind the barn, kissing. They never noticed me at all, though my path took me right past them.

Emily came over one afternoon to help me dress for a recital at school. She braided my hair and told me all about how wonderful Peter was. She was so happy. She seemed to glow as she tweaked the end of my braid and told me I was to be one of the attendants at her wedding. I was more pragmatic in nature, and said cautiously: "What do your parents think of him? He doesn't have the best reputation, you know."

Emily just laughed. "They will love him, just as I do," she said.

I wasn't so sure. Emily's father usually frowned when he saw Peter enter the parlor, and her mother had a worried look these days that I had never seen before.

"I'm going to tell them tonight," Emily said. "Peter wanted to be there, but I thought it was best if I broke the news first."

Smart Peter, I thought, but did not say so aloud.

"Why the rush?" I asked instead. "You've only known each other a few weeks."

"Well." Emily blushed a bit. "Can you keep a secret?"

Remembering the scene behind the barn, I knew at once what it was.

"You're in the family way," I said.

Emily nodded. "Peter wants to get married right away. So do I." She tugged the end of my braid once again. "Wish me luck," she said and went down the stairs and back to her home.

On our way to the recital, my brothers and I passed Emily's house. Even from the road we could hear her father yelling. Things were not going well for Emily, I thought. I wondered if she was going to tell them about the baby.

"Emily's pa sure is mad about something," said my eldest brother, Tim, who was escorting us to the recital. Tim had taken over the farm and the raising of us children after our pa died. He hurried us past Emily's house as quickly as he could. "I wonder if it has anything to do with that Peter fellow who's been beauing Emily lately. He's supposed to be a bad egg. I hear he came here to visit his cousins because he got some girl in the family way back home and then refused to marry her. Her family made it too hot for him to stay in town so he made a run for it. I hope Emily's all right."

Uh-oh, I thought.

I was getting ready for bed after my recital when a soft tap sounded on my door. Emily slipped in. She was wearing her traveling cloak and carrying a small bag.

"I just came to say good-bye," she said quietly. "You probably heard what Papa said tonight?"

I nodded.

"I think the whole town heard," she said with a sigh. "Well, I sent young Jimmy from the store with a note to Peter telling him what Papa said, and Peter sent me a note back saying to meet him tonight. We're going away to be married."

Remembering the other girl, I said: "Emily, don't. Peter doesn't have the best reputation. Tim said there was another girl back home . . ."

"I know all about it," she interrupted. "Peter explained the whole thing. Her beau got her in the family way, and when he skipped town she blamed Peter instead, hoping that her parents would force him to marry her. This is a completely different situation."

"Did you tell your parents you were in the family way?" I asked.

"Of course not!" Emily was shocked. "Papa would have killed Peter. Of course, Papa is going to disown me when he learns I eloped with Peter. But I don't care! Papa and Mama don't know anything about being in love."

I argued quietly with her for several more moments, but nothing I said swayed her decision. Finally she tweaked my braid, kissed me on the cheek, and slipped away.

I sat for a long time, trying to decide what to do. Perhaps Peter was serious about Emily and intended to do the right thing. Or perhaps he would skip town and Emily would be forced to go back home and tell her family her predicament. Some of her other beaus were so smitten with her that her family could easily find her a husband and hush the whole thing up.

I gave up trying to reason it out and went to talk to Tim. He was just about the smartest man in the world, and he would know what to do. Tim heard me out, and then said: "I know for a fact that Peter was the one who got that girl in trouble. We'd better go talk to Emily's folks."

Emily's pa was not happy to be wakened from a sound sleep. He was even more unhappy when he heard my story and saw for himself that Emily was gone. I could not tell him where Peter had arranged to meet Emily, since I did not know myself.

"Well, let's try to keep this quiet," he said finally. "Perhaps we can muddle through without a scandal." He looked suddenly old and weary.

My brothers and Emily's father and uncle spent most of the night searching for her. It was dawn, and I was milking the cows before breakfast when Tim came and told me Emily had hanged herself from the rafters of Gold Brook Bridge. Peter had left her a note saying he could not marry her. They'd found it clutched in her hand when they cut her down.

I leaned my head against the cow's side and cried like a baby.

It was about a month later that I first heard strange reports about the Gold Brook Bridge being haunted. A visitor to Stowe stood in the center of town, claiming that something had clawed his horse and carriage as he was crossing the covered bridge the night before. He had, he declared, heard a woman laughing angrily just before it happened. He offered to show the scratches on his new carriage to any skeptics. Tim went right over and felt the carriage. The scratches were definitely there.

Soon others reported that they, too, heard the sound of a woman's voice as they were crossing the bridge. More carriages and horses were clawed. Strange lights would appear and disappear all around the bridge after dark. People began saying that Emily's ghost was haunting the bridge.

I was very upset the first time I heard this. The Emily I knew would never hurt anyone. But of course, the Emily I knew was the young girl running away to meet her soul mate, not the young girl who was jilted by her lover and had hanged herself in despair.

Then a school friend of mine came to class one morning looking pale and upset. He and his pa had been driving across the bridge the night before when they were stopped by a pale figure that glowed in the darkness. It had taken all his father's strength to keep the terrified horses from bolting. The ghost had circled the cart slowly and then gripped the side next to my school friend and shook the carriage savagely. My friend's pa lost his hold on the horses, and they bolted across the bridge and ran so hard and fast that it took his pa several miles of frantic pulling to bring them to a halt. The ghostly figure, my friend said, glancing at me and then away, looked like Emily.

At dusk I walked down to the covered bridge. I told Tim where I was going and why, and he promised to come look for me if I wasn't back in an hour. I shivered as I walked into the darkness of the covered bridge. The sound of the babbling brook filled my ears. It took a few minutes for my eyes to adjust to the dim light. I leaned back against a wall and said quietly: "Emily?"

All I could hear was the rushing of water below the bridge. "Emily, I'm so sorry about Peter." The tears were trickling down my cheeks. "I tried to tell you about Peter. If only you had listened! I didn't want you to die." I was sobbing now, my hand over my mouth. I drew in a few gasping breaths and continued: "We didn't get to you quick enough. I should have hurried after you and made you stop. Please don't be angry with me."

I buried my face into my hands, overcome with guilt and pain. And somebody tugged on my braid. I stopped crying, shocked. I looked up and saw Emily standing beside me. She

EMILY'S BRIDGE

turned toward the entrance to the bridge and her face hardened. She clenched her fist and shook it. Then she looked back at me and her face softened. She leaned over and kissed my cheek, just as she had done the night she died. I felt the faintest prickling on my skin where her lips touched me. Then she was gone.

Tim came onto the bridge and took me by the hand. I wiped away my tears and said: "Do you think she will keep haunting this bridge?"

"Probably," said Tim. "Emily has a lot of anger to work out. But she's not mad at you. I wish you had told me what you told Emily. I would have set you straight. You did everything right that night. No one could have done better. Even Emily thinks so. She just proved it."

The bridge echoed with a familiar chuckle, and someone tugged my braid again.

"Good-bye, Emily," I said.

Tim and I went home.

11

The White Deer

The white deer was first seen drinking from Lake Onota by a warrior of the Housatonic tribe. He was amazed by the purity of the animal, which was completely white with no blemish upon her. Deciding she must be a sacred animal, blessed by the Great Spirit, the warrior hurried to bring the news to the chiefs of his tribe.

The chiefs swiftly declared that no arrow was ever to be pointed at this sacred deer. A prophecy was made about the white deer, which promised that as long as she came to drink from Lake Onota, pestilence, famine, and foe would never come to their land.

Living thus in the protection of the Indians, who threatened swift vengeance on any who tried to harm her, the white deer returned each year to drink from the lake. Good luck came to all who saw her, and doubly blessed was the Indian maiden who first laid eyes on the white deer in the spring. The year the white deer brought with her a pure white fawn was the most fruitful and happy the tribe had ever known.

But then the first French and Indian War broke out, and a French officer named Montalbert was sent to the Housatonic

Indians to enlist their aid against the English. Montalbert was fascinated by the story of the white deer. It was then the habit of adventurers in the New World to bring a trophy to the sovereign of their land, in exchange for which they were vastly rewarded. Montalbert determined that he would bring the pelt of the white deer to King Louis.

Montalbert promptly offered a great reward for the hunter who brought him the skin of the white deer. This horrified the chiefs, and Montalbert was quickly made to understand that a repetition of his offer would ensure him the fate he had planned for the white deer. Montalbert quickly offered his apologies, but he had made up his mind to have the white deer, and so he began to search for another way to attain the coveted prize. He did not have to search very far.

He discovered that an Indian named Wondo was overly fond of the white man's "firewater." Montalbert set about enslaving him with the continued application of spirits until Wondo would do anything to earn another drink. So Montalbert made the skin of the white deer his price for more firewater. Wondo was appalled by Montalbert's proposition, but his addiction was too strong, and at last he yielded to the will of the Frenchman.

The white deer, at home among the men of the tribe, never sensed her danger until it was too late. She was speedily brought to ground by the unhappy Wondo. As soon as the white pelt was in his possession, Montalbert set out posthaste for the safety of Montreal.

But Wondo, having exhausted his supply of firewater, miserably confessed his terrible crime to the chiefs of the tribe. Retribution was swift and merciless for the enslaved Wondo.

THE WHITE DEER

Then the warriors made haste after Montalbert, hoping that the destruction of the traitorous Frenchman would appease the Great Spirit.

Though Montalbert never made it to Montreal, and the skin of the white deer never graced the throne of King Louis, the Great Spirit no longer blessed the Housatonic tribe. Their prosperity gone and their hearts broken, the tribe slowly faded away until it was no more than a memory.

But folks say if you walk beside the water at dawn, you might see the spirit of the white deer, which haunts the banks of Lake Onota to this day.

12

The Blank Signboard

GRANVILLE, MASSACHUSETTS

"Storm's a-comin', Pa," Billy shouted as he raced into the kitchen.

"Boots," his mother yelled sternly, blocking his way to the taproom. "Unless you want to clean the floor?"

"Ah, Ma," Billy groaned, but he took off his boots and placed them by the back door. He slid across the wood floor in his stockings and into the bar.

"Pa!" he yelled.

James Taylor, the landlord of the inn, looked up from polishing the bar.

"I heard you, son. Half the town heard you. How bad a storm?"

"Old Chester says bad. Nor'easter. And it's gonna be snow, Pa. Couple days of it," said Billy.

Old Chester was the local weather-witch. Jimmy had known Old Chester all his life, and never once had Old Chester been wrong when he predicted the weather. Jimmy Taylor grinned. Bad storms were good for business. Peddlers and teamsters holed up at the inn during bad storms and spent lots of money.

Some of them would pay for room and board, all of them for shelter for their horses and for ale.

"Better clean out the barn," he told Billy. "The teamsters won't be expecting snow in November. They are all still using their wagons, and they are going to hightail it here quick when the snow starts."

"Or be stuck in a blizzard for three days!" Billy said gleefully.

"The barn," Jimmy reminded him. "Get your sister to help. And old Janet."

"I need Janet to finish getting the upstairs rooms turned out," Martha Taylor said from the kitchen. "And Rachel is on her way to the store for some extra groceries."

"Send Rachel to the barn when she gets back," said Jimmy. "Scoot, Billy. There are a great number of teamsters on the road right now, and they will need every space in the barn."

As Billy raced off, Jimmy continued: "Martha, I want you to keep old Janet out of the bar if you can. She is always eyeing the men. Young Stuart claims she pinched him last week."

"Well, at her age, she has to take her fun where she can," Martha said indulgently.

"I won't have her pinching the customers," Jimmy replied before heading down into the cellar. He was going to need to bring up a lot more ale.

Three hours before sunset, the nor'easter roared in. It started with hail and sleet, but quickly changed to thick snow. It was only November, but the snow fell as heavily as ever it did in January. The taproom of the Buxton Inn filled rapidly as teamsters, peddlers, and other travelers sought shelter from what looked to be a storm of several days' duration.

Both Billy and Rachel had to join Jimmy in the bar to help meet the continuous demand for drinks and food. After the first rush, Jimmy stood beside the tap polishing the glasses and beaming with delight. It was a full house, and that meant extra meat in the pot and maybe new shoes for Rachel.

Already the customers, mostly teamsters as he had predicted, were bored. With nothing to do until the snow stopped, the men sat around the bar, gambling and drinking. By the end of this storm, even those teamsters who slept for free around the fire and ate food from their wagons would have spent nearly all their money on ale and beer. Jimmy was a very happy man.

"Bartender, more beer!" shouted Red Ned Kelly, a huge teamster with a full red beard and an Irish brogue. "A toast to my friend Simon. Seems he forgot to put the runners on his wagon! Can't run a wagon in winter, Simon me lad! You need a sleigh to ride in snow."

"You should talk, Red," Simon retorted. "That 'sleigh' you parked out there has some mighty big wheels on it!"

The bar was noisy with laughter when someone began to pound on the front door of the inn. *Bang, bang, bang* went the iron knocker. Jimmy thought the door would break before he could get it open.

"Careful," he cried angrily, flinging the door open. A gust of snow made him stagger a bit as a fine gentleman swept into the room. Jimmy slammed the door shut as the gentleman shook the snow off his cloak with a debonair air. Underneath his cloak was a handsome suit with gold lace at the neck and sleeves—though Jimmy, who had an eye for such things, noted that his clothes were not of the latest fashion.

"Innkeeper!" he cried imperiously. Jimmy hastened forward.

"What sort of establishment is this?" the man raged. "There was no one outside to care for my horses! The path to the door is not even shoveled! I had to fight my way through waist-high snow while my servants were putting the horses and the sleigh in the barn. Even now, they are warming themselves by a fire while I stand here waiting to be served."

"Come in, good master. We have hot food ready now and a private parlor if you wish it," Jimmy said placatingly. "Rachel," he shouted to his daughter, who had taken over for him at the bar, "get this gentleman a drink."

"I will stay in the bar with the good people of this town," the man said grandly.

"Good people of this town! That's us, lads!" shouted Red Ned. "Come over and drink with us, then."

"Gladly," said the gentleman, to Jimmy's surprise. The stranger gracefully accepted a mug of ale from Rachel, who bobbed him a curtsy before returning to her place behind the bar. Striding over to the table near the fire, he took a seat between Simon and Red Ned and downed his ale in one gulp.

"More ale," he shouted.

Jimmy filled a pitcher with ale for the gentleman and placed it beside his elbow. The gentleman nodded his thanks without interrupting his story. Soon the table erupted with laughter, and there was a general call for more drinks.

The teamsters and peddlers were a bit awed by the gentleman's fine clothes and manners, but he soon put them at ease. Before long the bar was filled with singing, storytelling, smoking, and laughing. The fine gentleman seemed to be at the center of the activity.

"How about some dice then, lads?" Red Ned said after the last, and most ridiculous, set of tall tales was finished.

It was very late, but quite a number of men agreed to a game, including the strange gentleman. They retired to a back corner of the bar where they could signal the landlord for drinks without waking the sleepers around the fire.

Jimmy had sent the children to bed hours ago, but he remained in the bar, reluctant to lose any of the money the gamblers might spend on drinks. He went back to polishing glasses as he watched the gaming.

The stakes were low, and at first everyone seemed to have equal parts of good and bad luck. But then the gentleman started winning. Game after game the luck went one way, and with each win the gentleman became more arrogant, lording his triumph over the simple teamsters.

After two hours of rounds, the gentleman had a heap of the teamsters' coins in front of him while Red Ned had lost most of his cash. Sobered by his losses, and rather angry at the gentleman's attitude, Red Ned declared his intention to go to bed. The other teamsters, also irritated, agreed.

"So soon?" jeered the gentleman. "The night is still young!"

As if to prove him wrong, old Janet the housemaid came thumping into the bar to begin her morning round of work. As the gamblers rose and stretched, she pinched out the candles, cleared the glasses and mugs, and gradually made her way toward the group around the fire. The gentleman gathered his pennies and shillings, and with a triumphant gesture filled a red-velvet moneybag with his winnings.

As the man rose from his seat, he caught Janet's eye. She turned toward him, her eyes gleaming. Jimmy snapped to attention. The last thing he needed was to have Janet cause a scene by pinching the man.

But Janet stopped suddenly in surprise. "Why, sir," she said. "You are the image of Sir Charles!"

The gentleman looked at her with a cheeky smile. "And who might you be?"

"I am Janet, the housemaid, sir," she said, bobbing a curtsy.

"And this gentleman to whom you refer?"

"Sir Charles is the man pictured on our signboard," Jimmy broke into the conversation, keeping one eye on Janet's hands.

"The gentleman on the signboard, eh?" said the man. "Well, let's see how he looks! Innkeeper, where is the best place to view your signboard?"

Jimmy gestured to a window in the tavern parlor. The young gentleman swaggered over to the window, followed closely by Red Ned and several of the other teamsters, who had grown interested in the conversation. The dim early morning light and the blowing snow did not make for easy viewing of the signboard. But after squinting at it for several long moments, Red Ned said: "I don't see any portrait. The sign looks blank to me."

"Blank?" said Jimmy. He hurried to the window and glanced up at the sign. It *was* blank.

"How in blazes . . ." he began.

"For shame, innkeeper. Letting your portrait get away from you," the gentleman mocked from behind them. "Perhaps I can remedy the situation."

The men turned to look at the young blade. Jimmy blinked suddenly. The man seemed to be flickering in and out of focus.

THE BLANK SIGNBOARD

He really was the image of the missing portrait of Sir Charles, Jimmy realized. And then the man vanished.

Around him the teamsters exclaimed in wonder and fright. Had the man been a ghost? Jimmy turned back to the window and looked up at the signboard. And there was Sir Charles, back where he belonged. But there was something different about the picture. Jimmy stared at it in wonder, and then realized that peeking from Sir Charles's pocket was a bulging red-velvet bag. And in his hand, Sir Charles now held a shiny shilling.

13

The Image of Saint Francis

SWANTON, VERMONT

The Abenaki tribe were settling in for a good night's sleep following the wedding of the chief's eldest son in September 1759. So when the attack came, they were completely unprepared. The first shots came out of the blue, as 200 Rogers's Rangers swept down upon the defenseless town of Saint Francis. The soldiers killed and burned without mercy, their shouts vicious, their actions brutal.

Woken from their slumbers by the terrible sounds of gunshots and slaughter, men, women, and children fled in every direction. Those unfortunate folk who ran to the river were picked off before they could swim to the far shore. Many more were shot down in the street as they ran about in a daze. Two of the Rangers, Farrington and Bradley, broke into the home where the wedding had taken place and slaughtered everyone inside.

The village priest, a holy French Jesuit who daily summoned his charges to Mass, was awakened from his slumber by the screams. He hurried into the chapel and found many members of his parish taking refuge behind the altar. A few had lit candles and were praying to the image of Saint Francis for mercy.

Quickly donning the robes of his calling, the priest placed himself between the altar and the front door of the chapel, arms crossed upon his breast.

Outside, the sounds of slaughter and chaos were getting louder. The priest heard the Rangers shouting on the other side of the chapel door. The door shuddered under the blows of musket butts, and suddenly the room was filled with armed men.

The Rangers paused uncertainly on the threshold and gazed at the priest, who boldly placed himself between them and the people of his parish. Behind him the beautiful gold and silver holy vessels standing upon the altar were shimmering in the candlelight, but the faces of the women and children were filled with terror. The tribesmen gripped their weapons and glared menacingly at the invading Rangers, but stayed behind their priest, in whom they had the utmost faith.

Bradley, who had seen the group of Rangers entering the chapel, burst through the door and came face to face with the priest. Seeing the defiant tribesmen behind the altar, he immediately raised his rifle. The priest held out his arms in a gesture of supplication and said: "For the sake of Him who died on the Cross, stay your hand. Bring not this violence into the house of God."

"Hear him," laughed one of the Rangers. "He gabbles worse than a flock of geese."

The men all laughed. The Rangers scorned the Catholic Church and her missionaries who worked among the "savages." They considered the priest to be the real head of the tribe, and thus hated him.

"Yield, Papist, and I give you my word as a Ranger that you shall live," said Bradley.

"Never," said the priest, ignoring the muttered warning behind him. Bradley shook his head gravely. "I will ask you one more time, Father," he said in a very gentle voice.

The priest turned to the altar, caught up the silver image of Saint Francis, and held it above his head. "Behold the patron saint of this village. To your knees, monsters," he cried.

Bradley pulled the trigger and shot the priest through the heart. As he fell to the floor, the holy statue rolling away from his body, the other Rangers invaded the chapel, killing indiscriminately and claiming the holy gold and silver as their prize.

When all were dead, the men turned to leave through the front door. Behind them, from somewhere among the bodies heaped under the altar, a voice rose: "The Great Spirit of the Abenaki will scatter darkness in your paths," it said. "Hunger will walk among you. Death will strike you. Your wives will weep for their warriors who will never return. Manitou is angered by the voice of the dead. He will bring this to pass."

To a man, the Rangers froze in their tracks. Then Bradley offered an uncertain laugh and pushed the men out the door. He set fire to the chapel, and the Rangers walked away from the rapidly burning village. As they picked their way through the ruins, the chapel bell began to toll. *Bong, bong, bong.* The bell rang slowly, the measured strokes sounding out a death knell that chilled all who heard it.

Although his men were exhausted after the atrocities of the night, Rogers could not afford to let them rest. More than 300 French and Indians were drawing closer by the hour, trailing the Rangers. So the Rangers struck out through the rugged, forbidding forest. Not knowing the country, they were soon hopelessly lost. For three days, they wandered in circles through a dense swamp. By the third day all their provisions were gone, many of them sunk into the waters of the swamp. Hungry and exhausted, they did not dare hunt for food lest their enemies hear the gunshots.

Sheer luck brought them onto a trail behind the French and Indian troops. It was decided then to split the Rangers into nine groups. Each group would try to make its way separately to safety. If any encountered the enemy, they would give battle in order to allow the others to escape.

A short while after separating, the Rangers could hear the sound of repeated firing as one of the parties met the French and Indian troops head-on. Too soon, the sounds of battle ceased, and the members of the eight remaining parties knew their companions were dead.

But Manitou was not finished with the Rangers. The blood of 300 Abenaki and one holy priest was crying out for vengeance, and Manitou had heard the voice of the dead. The eight groups of Rangers wandered on, lost, starving, and afraid. The men started at shadows, ever fearful of their enemies, and fired blindly at nothing until their powder was gone. Unable to hunt, their water supply depleted, one by one the Rangers fell by the wayside to die. Some were too weak to utter a cry. Others begged God for mercy, haunted by the faces of their victims. Finally the remaining men took to devouring the corpses of the dead in order to survive.

In this manner the Rangers, their numbers reduced to a few handfuls, finally regrouped on the shores of the Memphremagog. Rogers had survived the brutal trip, and he constructed a raft and braved the dangerous journey down the river alone. He later returned with help for the pitiful remnants of his troops.

THE IMAGE OF SAINT FRANCIS

By the time the men reached their homes, the treasures of Saint Francis had all disappeared, and the Rangers who survived the trip were haunted the rest of their lives by the memories of the deeds they had done to survive.

For many years following the massacre, hunters would find signs of the terrible journey—rusty buttons, decayed cloth; once, two golden candlesticks were discovered on the shores of the Memphremagog. But the image of Saint Francis was never heard of again.

Many years later a hunter was wandering in the mountains near the ruined village of Saint Francis when he was overtaken by a terrific storm. Sheltering in a cave, the hunter watched the black clouds rolling and the lightning playing across the sky. Suddenly across the black clouds appeared the skeleton of an Indian, while above the raging of the storm rose the howls and screams of the lost. The hunter clasped his hands over his ears, afraid the sound would drive him mad. But then the mists rolled back, the storm ceased, and a gap appeared in the clouds.

A single ray of light burst across the mountaintop. In the silence a great stone church appeared, glowing in the ray of light. The doors of the church opened to reveal a beautiful altar, gold and silver holy vessels shimmering in the candlelight. Incense rose from a sparkling censer, and around the altar knelt the men, women, and children of Saint Francis. Then the church disappeared, and the hunter could see the people of the town marching solemnly up the steep mountain trail, following the glittering silver image of Saint Francis. The Blessed Virgin Mary appeared at the top, arms open to welcome them. Then clouds covered the gap in the sky, and the vision was gone.

14

The Whaling Boat in the Sky

ORLEANS, MASSACHUSETTS

The wind was whipping fiercely across the bay and storm clouds were boiling in the sky when Captain Southack ordered his whaling boat out of the harbor. At any other time he would have kept his men ashore rather than face a nor'easter, but this was his one chance to intercept the pirate Bellamy, and Captain Southack was determined to take it.

Black Sam Bellamy, the scourge of the West Indies, was Captain Southack's personal nemesis. Bellamy was the captain of a notorious band of pirates who had attacked and plundered more than fifty ships. Captain Southack was determined to apprehend Samuel Bellamy at any cost.

The "prince" of pirates had been following the coastline north during the early months of spring in this year of our Lord 1717, plundering any vessels he encountered. A dashing Englishman who usually wore a velvet coat with four pistols tucked into his sash, Black Sam ignored the fashion of powdering his long black hair, choosing instead to wear it tied back with a black bow. But Captain Southack knew this dashing man was a thief and a killer and so despised him.

The captain had heard it speculated that the scurrilous crew was heading to Richman Island, off the coast of Maine. But Southack thought he knew a better place to intercept the pirate. Bellamy apparently had a mistress, one Maria Hallet, who lived in Eastham out near the tip of Cape Cod. Bellamy had promised Maria that he would return for her, sailing the longest, tallest ship she had ever seen.

Just a few months ago, Bellamy had captured the *Whydah*, a fabulous hundred-foot, three-masted galley, and had claimed her as his flagship. The *Whydah* was filled with an incredible treasure of ivory, indigo, and thousands of silver and gold coins. Having attained his "long, tall ship," Southack was sure Samuel Bellamy would come ashore at Cape Cod to claim the hand of his mistress and sail away with her.

So Southack had prepared his ship and waited patiently for news of the pirates' approach. Such news had finally arrived, and nothing, not even a terrible April nor'easter, would deter Captain Southack from his pursuit of the pirate.

The sturdy whaling boat swayed fiercely as she met the large swells. The howl of the approaching storm made the crew nervous.

The first mate approached Southack warily. "Captain," he said, "the storm is getting closer. We will never find Bellamy in this weather."

"We will find Bellamy. I will chase him down if I have to sail to hell and back," the captain said coldly.

"From the looks of those clouds, you might not be far off the mark," muttered the first mate, turning away from his superior's grim face. The mate shouted to the men to prepare the storm sail and batten down the hatches.

The wind was in their favor, and they were making good time across the bay when the storm broke. Thunder rumbled, lightning flashed across the sky, and the boat was enveloped by a blinding rain. The waves rose higher and higher. The wind was gusting close to seventy miles per hour.

"Captain, we must turn back," shouted the first mate.

"Never," cried Southack. "We have but one chance to capture Bellamy, and we must take it."

"But Captain," yelled the mate over the thunderous rain, "we cannot see the Cape. We will run aground."

The waves tossed the whaling boat about like a toy, but the captain gave the order to continue as best they could against the mountainous waves. He knew that they could not turn back now, even if they had wished it. They were running blind in the storm. The heavy rain and fog made it impossible to see more than a few feet beyond the ship.

"Breakers off the port bow," shouted the lookout suddenly. The captain took the wheel and yanked the whaling boat to starboard. The first mate had several members of the crew tie themselves to the rail so they wouldn't be lost when they leaned over it to try to see how close they were to shore. But the rain and the fog were so dense that none of the men could see anything.

Following their close call with the breakers, the captain noticed that the waves buffeting the boat were no longer as high or fierce. Still, the vessel felt as if it were in the grip of a strong current. All he could do was clutch the wet wheel and pray.

"Captain," the first mate called over the roar of the wind and rain. "Some of the crew have reported seeing tall, shadowy forms in the mist. They looked a bit like trees. Is it an omen?"

"Tell the men to hold on and pray," Captain Southack said grimly.

They were gripped by the strange current for what seemed like hours. The wind and rain still beat fiercely on the whaling boat, but the sense of being sheltered somehow would not leave the captain. Once, a crewman ran up to the first mate, babbling wildly. The captain could not make out what he said to the mate, the roar of the storm being too loud, and he dared not leave the wheel or even look away for longer than a moment. He thrust his wet hair away from his straining eyes and beckoned with one hand to the first mate.

"What was that about?" he called over the storm.

"Jones thought he saw a house among the waves," the first mate yelled.

"A house?" the captain asked, astonished.

"I think the strain is getting to him," said the first mate. "If we didn't need all hands on deck, I'd send him below."

The captain nodded.

"Breakers," the lookout sang out suddenly, echoed by excited cries from the men at the rail.

"Where?" shouted the captain.

"Port."

"Starboard."

Both cries came at once.

"Keep her steady as she goes," the lookout shouted frantically. "We may be able to ride this next wave over the breakwater."

The captain's grip tightened on the wheel until his knuckles were white. He kept her steady, feeling the wave swelling beneath the ship. A moment later they were past the breakwater and climbing a mountainous wave. The wind hit the whaling boat with a fierceness that had previously been missing as the ship slid down the other side of the massive wave. Whatever had been sheltering the ship was no longer there. The captain did not know whether to be glad or sorry. Jones's story of a house made him nervous. And several others had reported seeing shadows that looked like trees . . .

The captain jerked his attention back to the wheel, telling himself not to be foolish.

The storm gave out at last, and the exhausted captain and his crew looked around them, trying to see where the storm had taken their ship.

Timidly, the first mate approached Southack. "Captain," he said slowly. "Captain, we're not in the bay."

"What do you mean, we're not in the bay?" snapped the exhausted man.

"I mean we just took a sounding. Captain, we're in the Atlantic. And I would swear that the land over yonder is the shore of Cape Cod."

And so it was. Somehow, the whaling boat had made its way into the Atlantic.

"Make for shore," the captain told his mate wearily. As the whaling boat made its way back to shore, Southack noticed a wide river coursing through the trees and down to meet the waves. Breakers burst on every side of the current.

The first mate noticed it, too. "Captain," he gasped. "Captain! That's where we came out last night! We must have sailed right over the Cape."

They went ashore at Orleans, where the crew learned that the first mate's guess was correct. During the storm, the seas had

THE WHALING BOAT IN THE SKY

risen thirty feet with waves as high as forty feet, and a temporary river, down which several residents had seen the whaling boat sailing, had coursed across the meadows of Orleans.

As for Bellamy, his treasure-laden ship had been trapped in the surf near the beach off Cape Cod and had broken apart on a sandbar. The ship had been rolled by a giant wave and split in two, spilling the treasure across the ocean floor. The locals found more than a hundred mutilated corpses near the wreck. There were only two survivors; neither of them was Bellamy.

Captain Southack was sent to recover as much treasure as he could, and to try to stop the plundering of the wreck. One of the survivors, a Welshman named Davis, testified at his trial in Boston that the *Whydah* had contained more than three million dollars' worth of gold, silver, and jewels. The majority of the treasure was never found.

Bellamy's mistress, Maria Hallet, was later accused of being a witch and cast out of Eastham. She died young, and her spirit still walks the cliffs near the wreck. As for Captain Southack's incredible journey across the Cape—well, the locals in Orleans still like to tell the tale. And just before a storm, a mirage appears in the sky above Orleans. It is Captain Southack's whaling boat, sailing once again across the meadows of Orleans in pursuit of the pirate Bellamy.

15

The Dancing Mortar

BLOCK ISLAND, RHODE ISLAND

It looked like just an ordinary mortar—the kind you use to grind corn with a pestle. Mortars just like it were common in communities that didn't have a mill. It was a rectangular box around fourteen inches high and ten inches in diameter. The wood was stone-hard lignum vitae, made from logs dropped off on Block Island by the *Palatine* after a voyage from the West Indies. Perhaps it would have remained a plain old mortar if it hadn't been kept in the Simon Ray house.

Now, Simon Ray owned a large old house on Block Island. Into this house he had welcomed many of the sick and needy travelers left off on Block Island by the *Palatine*. When travelers died, he gave them a Christian burial in a private graveyard near his house. Simon was much praised for the compassion he showed these poor folk.

The first sign of something amiss at the Ray house was reported by the town drunk, so no one took him seriously when he said that as he passed the home late one night, a banshee had screeched at him from the top of the old pines. "Scared me sober," he declared. His statement, delivered in an advanced state of inebriation, brought a round of laughter from the townsfolk at the tavern.

But soon some of the more reputable citizens began reporting that strange things had happened to them when they passed the Ray house. The island doctor was pelted with rotten apples as he left the front door after attending a patient. But the apples were of a kind that did not grow anywhere on the island. The minister was accosted at the gate by a shimmering, twisting mist that spoke to him in a deep, guttural voice of things he grew pale to hear and would never repeat.

And the reports kept coming. A voice wailing among the treetops. Lights appearing and disappearing in the lane and down the road. Missiles hurling themselves at passersby. The locals thought the ghosts of the men buried in the graveyard nearby were haunting the house. But it soon became apparent that the culprit must be a hobgoblin. Strangely, the Ray family never heard or saw anything. The hobgoblin left them alone.

Then one night after dinner, when the family and their guests were gathered around the huge fireplace in the parlor, the mortar, which was sitting on a table next to the wall, suddenly threw itself on its side, striking the table with a hollow thump. Then it rose up into the air, untouched by human hands, and landed with a thud on the wooden floor. Mistress Ray, a plump, pretty woman in her early forties, uttered a terrified shriek. Her guests gave a concerted gasp, and the mothers drew their children into their arms away from the alarming sight.

But the mortar was not through. It began to roll from one side of the room to the other, making a loud *clack-a-clack* sound as its square sides whacked the floor. Some devilish impulse seemed to propel the mortar right toward the watchers. Men, women, and children dodged out of the path of the haunted mortar, afraid its touch might infect them with the witchery that possessed it. Mistress Ray leapt to the top of her chair and began a steady wailing that almost drowned out the clacking of the mortar as it played tag with the guests.

The noise brought Simon Ray running in from the back door, where he had been cleaning his shoes after putting his horse in the barn. He saw his pretty wife on the chair and had started toward her when the mortar came rolling right up to his feet and then pushed itself upright. Simon's mouth dropped open.

"What the h—?" He stopped, remembering there were ladies and children present. "What is happening here?"

The mortar gave a little hop and then began to dance across the floor again, bouncing from corner to corner, getting higher with each bounce until it was bouncing across the joists on the ceiling, hopping on the furniture, whirling around the room. Simon grabbed his wife off the chair. He flung her and then himself out an open window into the summer night, thankful that the parlor was on the ground floor. They landed with a thump in the hedges outside the window. Behind them, the guests remaining in the room poured themselves through all the available doors and windows.

Peeking back into the window he had just exited, Simon saw the mortar dancing alone across the ceiling and the floor. After a few moments it hopped back onto the table where it usually stood and went still.

"What is it doing now?" his wife asked at his shoulder.

"It has stopped," Simon said. Through the window, he saw that his guests were slowly moving back into the parlor, talking

THE DANCING MORTAR

excitedly. He turned to his wife. "Well, my dear, it seems the good people in town are right. We have a hobgoblin."

It did not take long for word to spread about the dancing mortar. Even the townsfolk who had encountered the hobgoblin were skeptical at first. People took to dropping in at the Ray house right after dinner with trumped-up excuses to look at the mortar. They were disappointed at its ordinary appearance. The tale would have been dismissed out of hand if the mortar hadn't started to dance on a Sunday afternoon when the Rays had the minister and his wife over for dinner. The minister stood in the middle of the parlor with his Bible and prayed aloud over the bewitched mortar, but it just danced away to some inner music of its own.

After that the Rays found themselves besieged with visitors hoping to see the mortar dance. Even the howls, wails, and missiles of the hobgoblin became a source of wonder rather than fear. Soon the haunted Ray house and the dancing mortar became a folk legend on the island; visitors would stop by the house of an evening hoping to have a supernatural encounter.

As the years passed, the antics of the hobgoblin and dancing mortar became intermittent, and then ceased all together. Simon Ray's descendants turned the mortar out of doors, where it was used as a splitting block for the woodpile—it being nearly as hard as stone. Finally the old Ray house was torn down and a new one erected a few hundred yards away. The new owner, Raymond Dickens, used some of the wood from the old house to build the new, but being acquainted with the story of the mortar, he had it placed in a wall, weighed down with heavy stones so it would never dance again.

16

You Can't Get Out

HARTFORD, CONNECTICUT

I sat at the bar, nursing my beer and watching as Eddie Johnson came through the door. He called general greetings to his friends as he weaved his way through the smoky room and sat down on the opposite side of the bar.

"What'll it be, Eddie?" asked Joseph, as if he didn't already know.

"Just a soda for me, Joe," Eddie said. Around some of the tables, men were nodding knowingly to each other. But Bart, who was visiting from the next village, stared at Eddie in disbelief. Eddie was known in three counties for his incredible drinking capacity.

"A soda?" Bart asked in shock. "Eddie, what happened to you? I never heard you order soda before!"

There was a familiar gleam in Eddie's eyes when he looked at the out-of-town chap. Eddie loved to tell folks the story of how he came to be sober. And everyone in town loved to hear it. Conversations all over the room came to an abrupt halt as Eddie moved down the bar to sit next to Bart.

"Well, Bart, I ain't had a drink in over three months," Eddie began. "My missus was after me to give up drinking. She always

97

said the Devil would drag me right down to Hell if I didn't mend my ways. But I wouldn't listen to her. No sir, I was the first one in the bar and the last one out most every night."

"I remember," said Bart. "What happened?"

Everyone in the tavern leaned forward to listen as Eddie told his tale.

One dark, windy night last summer Eddie was walking home from the bar and got lost. He'd had a tad too much to drink and got himself turned around—couldn't figure out which way was home. The night was pitch-black, and Eddie couldn't see his hand in front of his face. Somehow, he made his way into the churchyard and found himself in the cemetery. He was sure he was in the cemetery on account of all the crosses and stones with fancy carvings on them.

Ah, ha! Eddie thought to himself. *I know how to get home now!*

As he walked through that cemetery, a strong breeze picked up and started howling around his head. He could hear creepy voices in that wind, moaning, "Eddie . . . Eddie . . ." Skin crawling and hands as cold as ice, Eddie started hurrying homeward as fast as he could, eager to leave the dark cemetery.

Suddenly, the ground opened up in front of him. Eddie stopped short, barely managing to keep his balance without falling into the hole. Then a skeletal hand reached up and wrapped itself around his leg. Eddie gave a shout and tried to break away, but the hand tripped him and pulled him down into the hole.

Eddie fell a long, long way. Finally, he landed on the bottom with a tremendous thump that knocked the breath right out of him. The wind blew harder and harder, filling that deep hole with swirling air. Unearthly voices kept moaning his name:

"Eddie . . . Eddie . . ." and the skeletal hand gripped his leg so hard he thought his bones would break. Eddie knew then that the Devil had come for him; come to take him down to Hell because of all his drinking, just like his wife had said.

Suddenly, the hand gripping his leg loosened up. It started to glow from the inside. Backing up against the wall, Eddie watched as the skeleton hand rose into the air. A robe formed around the skeleton hand and became a glowing specter of death that stared down at Eddie with fathomless, empty eyes. It had a ghastly skull that filled the hood.

"Eddie . . . Eddie . . ." the wind moaned as it leaked around the terrible figure before him. Then a voice came from the skull of the specter.

"You can't get out!" the specter intoned in the deep, intense tones of the dead. "You can't get out."

"God save me!" Eddie cried in fear.

Suddenly, he was filled with a miraculous strength that could have come only from heaven itself. Giving a great leap, Eddie reached for the top of the hole. The specter made a grab for his leg, but he avoided it and scrambled up to the top. The unearthly breeze tried to knock Eddie back into the hole, but he started singing "Glory Hallelujah," and his song cut right through those moaning voices. Then Eddie was free and running for home.

"And I haven't had a drink from that day to this," Eddie said, concluding his tale. "God saved me from the Devil and I ain't never going back. I've started going to church every Sunday with me wife, and now she's the happiest woman in town. I've been given a second chance, Bart, and I don't mean to waste it."

Bart was pop-eyed with amazement. He was so impressed with the tale that he bought Eddie another soda and even drank one himself.

Now that the story was over, the other men in the bar started talking amongst themselves—all except old Tom Miller, who was sitting at a corner table, shaking with silent laughter. I was intrigued. I thought that Eddie's story was terrifying and inspiring, but not funny. Why was the old man laughing? I took my beer over and joined him at the table.

"Why are you laughing, Tom Miller?" I asked.

Tom let out a happy cackle. "Can't tell you, Fred. It's a secret," he said.

"Come on, Tom. You know I can keep a secret," I said.

I'd never told Tom's wife about the time he stole her ugly new apron to make a scarecrow. She still talked about the mystery whenever she came to visit with my wife.

Tom nodded. "Yep, I reckon you can." Then he told me another version of Eddie's tale.

Tom just happened to be taking the shortcut through the cemetery one dark and windy night last summer. And he fell right into a fresh-dug hole that was prepared for ol' Jeb Thompson's funeral the next day. It was a big, deep hole, and he couldn't get out, no matter how much he scrambled up the sides. The dirt kept crumbling under his hands. Tom figured he was stuck in there until morning. The mortician would be along pretty early, and he could fetch a ladder to get Tom out.

About an hour later, Tom was napping at the bottom of the hole when he awoke to the sound of some loud, off-key singing. It was Eddie Johnson walking home from the bar. Eddie must have been real drunk, because he was all turned around and

YOU CAN'T GET OUT

kept trying to find his way home through the cemetery. Eddie's voice kept getting closer and closer. Tom yelled his name, hoping Eddie would help him out of the hole. But instead, Eddie fell into the grave, right on top of Tom.

Eddie scrambled around some and tried to climb out of the hole, just like Tom had. Finally, Tom said, "Eddie, you can't get out that way." And Eddie jumped straight up in the air. Tom had never seen anyone jump so high. Eddie did a little flip near the top of the hole, grabbed the edge, and was gone before Tom could say another word. Tom had been hoping they could boost each other out of the hole, but Eddie was already halfway home before Tom knew what had happened. So Tom had to wait until the mortician came in the morning to get out of the hole after all.

After the funeral, Tom heard Eddie telling some of his friends about the "specter in the graveyard." He was so sincere about quitting his drinking that Tom didn't have the heart to tell him the real story. "The mortician must have told Eddie's wife what really happened," Tom concluded, "because she baked me an apple pie and sent me a bouquet of her best roses to thank me!"

I laughed until the tears came to my eyes. Tom Miller swore me to secrecy, and I promised with a good will. Then I made my way out of the bar, pausing to thump Eddie on the shoulder and thank him for the fine example he was setting for the community. Eddie beamed at me and took another swig of soda.

"Thank you, Fred. I owe it all to God, who saved me from that terrible specter," he said piously.

What else could I say, but "Amen"?

17

Playin' Piano

Dah-dah-dum-dum-BLAT!

Charlie winced when his wife hit the wrong note on the piano for the thirty-second time that day. He knew it was the thirty-second time because he'd kept count as he went about his daily chores: cleaning the lighthouse, checking the supplies, mending the rowboat.

Charlie and his wife, Myrtle, lived on a small island off the coast of Maine. Charlie was the lighthouse keeper, and he worked hard to keep everything up-to-date, spankin' clean, and in perfect order. No ships were going to wreck on the local reef while he was in command of the lighthouse. Myrtle kept house and made crafts to sell at the local onshore market during their once-a-month trip into town.

Charlie and Myrtle had been married for almost ten years, and generally got along quite happily together, despite having no children. After she lost the first two, the doctor had told Myrtle that she wouldn't be able to have any more. Myrtle had taken the news stoically and had refused to adopt a child from the orphanage when Charlie proposed the idea. Still, Charlie suspected she really did feel the lack of motherhood in her life, and that it was probably the cause of her latest obsession.

Charlie blamed himself, really. He should never have taken Myrtle to attend the concert when that highfalutin concert pianist came to town. But it was a special occasion, and everyone they knew was going. So Charlie and Myrtle went, too. And Myrtle decided right then and there that what she wanted more than life itself was to play the piano.

Charlie tried to talk her out of it. No one in Myrtle's family was any good at music. Couldn't carry a tune in a bucket, the lot of them. In fact, when her Uncle Teddy played the fiddle, he cleared out the whole house. Even the neighbors went to town to escape the sound. Besides, Charlie argued, they couldn't possibly afford a piano. And how would they get it out to the island? Where would they fit one inside their small lighthouse?

But Myrtle was as stubborn as her Uncle Teddy. If she couldn't find a dad-gum way, she'd make one! Before Charlie could count to ten she'd bought a cheap, used piano (that was always out of tune) and hauled it over to the island on her brother Jamie's fishing boat. She would have kept it at the foot of their bed if Charlie hadn't drawn the line there. So Myrtle put Charlie's favorite rocking chair and table out in the woodshed and installed her piano in the main living space.

From that day on, it was practice, practice, practice. Morning, noon, and night Myrtle sat at the piano with her songbook open, plunking away at the keys. At first, there was not much to hear, and Charlie could ignore the sour sounds. But after a few months, she got better . . . and a lot worse. There were parts of her song that sounded pretty good; but she never, ever got that one line right. *Dah-dah-dum-dum-BLAT* went the piano, every time. Twelve weeks in a row she'd been playing the same song without any improvement. Sometimes she'd continue after the first *BLAT*, and that was even worse. *Dum-dum-BLAT-BLAT-ding!*

There was nowhere on the small island that Charlie could go to get away from the sound, even when he sat in his favorite rocker out in the woodshed with cotton in his ears. Myrtle's new hobby was the source of much contention between husband and wife, who had never argued before. Now they argued every day.

"At least try to learn another song," Charlie begged his wife. But Myrtle was stubborn.

"I ain't going to learn another song until I've mastered this one. You've got to practice to get better, Charlie."

"Your Uncle Teddy practices his fiddle every Saturday night," Charlie snapped, "and he hasn't gotten any better in fifty years."

But Myrtle refused to listen. She just went back to her piano and started playing again. *Dah-dah-dum-dum-BLAT / Dum-dum-BLAT-BLAT-ding.* Charlie went upstairs to polish the light. He put wax in his ears, but even that did not completely muffle the sound.

Things came to a head the day a nor'easter roared down on the island. Charlie and Myrtle were holed up together in the lighthouse hour after hour after hour. Charlie's chores were swiftly completed, and aside from regular checks on the light and a quick sweep of the beaches to make sure no ships were in danger, Charlie had nothing to do but sit and carve decoy ducks. And Myrtle played the piano. Hour after hour after hour. *Dah-dah-dum-dum-BLAT / Dum-dum-BLAT-BLAT-ding.*

Around 4 p.m. Charlie leapt to his feet and shouted at his wife to stop playing the blasted song. Myrtle leapt to her feet and shouted that she was going to practice until she got it right. After a brief but fierce argument, Myrtle sat down at the piano and started playing again. *Dah-dah-dum-dum-BLAT / Dum-dum-BLAT-BLAT-ding.*

Then something in Charlie snapped.

A little while later, he felt bad about the way he chopped up the piano with his ax. After all, it was a valuable instrument. Try as he might, though, he couldn't feel bad about doing the same to Myrtle.

Charlie put on his oilskins, took up a shovel, and dug a grave out back of the woodshed. He buried all the little pieces of Myrtle with all the little pieces of her piano. He figured she would have wanted it that way. Later that night, with the nor'easter raging and pounding the island, and the lighthouse rattling and shaking wildly in the blast, Charlie got the best sleep he'd had in months. No more piano playing, ever.

The nor'easter blew itself out sometime the next morning. The island was peaceful and quiet once again, with no music at all save for the lap of the waves and the soughing of the wind through the pine trees. Charlie spent the rest of the day cleaning the blood off the floor and walls of the lighthouse. After that, he did his daily duties, moved his favorite rocking chair and table back into the main room, and carefully noted in the logbook the terrible tragedy that had befallen his wife during the storm.

Myrtle, according to the log, had been swept out to sea by a huge wave while heroically patrolling the beaches, helping Charlie look for shipwrecks.

PLAYIN' PIANO

In the middle of the night, Charlie was startled awake by a familiar sound. *Dah-dah-dum-dum-BLAT / Dum-dum-BLAT-BLAT-ding.* He sat bolt upright with an oath. It sounded just like Myrtle playing on the piano. But that was impossible—she was buried behind the woodshed!

Charlie leapt out of bed and felt around for his ax. Blast! He must have left it in the woodshed. He picked up a large piece of firewood and carefully stepped through the door into the main room, while the piano played its sour tune again and again. Charlie stared in astonishment at the glowing green translucent piano that stood once again in the place where Myrtle had put it. He could see his rocking chair and the end table right through the dad-blame instrument, which was somehow contriving to share space with them. The keys of the ghostly piano were playing all by themselves. *Dah-dah-dum-dum-BLAT / Dum-dum-BLAT-BLAT-ding.*

Then he heard Myrtle's voice coming from the stairway leading up to the light. "Charlie, over and over I told you . . . I ain't going to learn another song until I've mastered this one. You should have listened to me!"

Charlie whirled around and gazed toward the stairs. Standing a third of the way up the spiral staircase was the translucent white figure of his dead wife. And in her hands, she held his ax.

18

Root Beer

There's always some crime around the time of the St. Johnsbury Fair. All kinds of reprobates crawl out of the woodwork—pickpockets and con men and such—trying to do the hardworking townsfolk out of their money. It comes with the territory, as they say. But this year felt different. Something wasn't right. We felt it as soon as we set foot on the fairgrounds, but it wasn't until my wife Helen and I encountered a couple of memorable chaps playing a "friendly card game" in the far corner of the fair that we knew the source of the tension in the air.

Helen and I stood and watched the game for a few moments from the outskirts. A chap named Andrew Barr was running the table. I was acquainted with most of the fellows sitting with him—nice enough folks, but none of them had much sense or they'd never have set foot at that table.

My wife nudged me and pointed to the chubby stranger sitting across from Andrew. The man's face was beaming and childlike, portraying a simple man just waiting to be cheated of all his coins. But somehow, the pile in front of him got larger, not smaller. I couldn't detect a signal passing between the chubby stranger and Andrew, yet somehow between them they wiped out the rest of the card players in two rounds.

When the first round of duped players left, the chubby fellow wandered away with them. Seeing our interest, he stopped to introduce himself—Frank Ballard, surveyor—and invite us to play a round with him. "I'm sure we can beat the dealer working together," he said jovially. But his eyes were hard behind the smile, and underneath his chubby outline he was all muscle. This man was a bully.

"I'm afraid we only brought enough money to buy some of Washburn's homemade root beer," my wife said with a sweet smile. "We don't have spare cash on hand these days, what with the hard winter. Unless you play for vegetables? I think we still have a bushel of tomatoes in the wagon, don't we, Henry?"

Frank lost interest as soon as Helen mentioned root beer and vegetables. He tipped his hat politely and went trotting after a prosperous-looking man in a suit. At the table, Andrew kept shuffling the cards and didn't look up as we wandered away.

Helen and I stopped by Washburn's cart next. Uriah and his boy Dabby were neighbors of ours. Dabby was born with clubfeet which caused him to walk with a limp, but he never let that stop him. He was a brilliant herbalist and made the best root beer in the county. We sat for several minutes chatting and watching the festive crowd strut around in their Sunday best as we drank two glasses each of Dabby's root beer. Then we headed back to our wagon to drive home so I could milk the cows before supper.

The fair ended soon enough, but the trouble did not. Andrew and Frank started wandering around from town to town, hanging out at taverns and general stores, pretending to be government surveyors. Tales of their adventures sounded more like the heroics of Hercules than the dull work usually assigned to those employed by Uncle Sam. Still, it gave folks something interesting to talk about besides the crime wave that was sweeping the county.

Break-ins were frequent that year. Nearly every family in town had lost money or livestock or goods of some kind. Andrew and Frank were often heard advising the latest victim on things they could do in the future to keep thieves away from their property. Folks thought it was right kind of them.

"It's amazing the way Frank and Andrew can spot the weak point in everybody's house," Helen said dryly. The following day she drove to the next county and purchased a couple of very large, very protective guard dogs from one of her cousins. In spite of our rather secluded location, our home was not broken into that winter.

Fair-time rolled around again, bringing a couple of new characters to town. Helen and I liked these fellows even less than Frank and Andrew. Terrance Blunt was another gambler, like Andrew. But his companion was not. Cal Longstreet was a ladies' man. As soon as I laid eyes on him, I was real glad my girls were all married and living in the next county. I didn't think any young lady was safe from such a man. Perhaps it was inevitable that all four of those nasty characters formed an unholy alliance. Anyone who gambled at their table walked away with empty pockets. They sat in the refreshments tent telling stories as fascinated listeners bought them ale and hard liquor.

During the first two weeks of the fair, a nasty crime wave suddenly swept through all the towns in the county. Houses were broken into; horses were stolen; people had their pockets picked. The local law enforcement put notices up everywhere, hoping to discourage the widespread crime. Then the unholy four got careless and several citizens came forward to testify against them. The notices were replaced with Wanted posters and pictures of the unholy four. Despite this increased attention, their crime wave continued unabated. Then three young women were killed; one right after another, they were violated and strangled with a long scarf. New Wanted signs were hammered into posts with an additional phrase: Dead or Alive.

On the last day of the fair, Helen found Dabby crying in the back of the wagon when we stopped by to purchase homemade root beer. His friend Tessie was one of the murdered girls, and Dabby was devastated by her loss. "Why? Why did this happen?" he asked Helen over and over. She had no answer for him.

That night, a huge storm descended on the town. Wind thrashed the trees, heavy rain blew sideways; lightning flashed, thunder roared. I tucked all our livestock into the snug barn for safekeeping with one of the dogs. Then I flew in the kitchen door and stuffed my wet outdoor things onto the coat rack before joining Helen beside the cozy fire. Boy howdy, was I glad to be indoors on such a terrible night.

I sat reading the newspaper all evening, lulled into a pleasant stupor by the pounding of the rain and the howl of the wind. I jerked awake from a light doze about an hour after my visit to the barn, my pulse pounding. I was sure that I heard the sound of a wagon driving past our house, although how I could hear anything over the storm was a mystery. I got up and peered out through the rain streaming down the window, but I could see nothing except lashing tree branches.

"What is it?" Helen asked, looking up from her knitting.

"I don't know," I replied uneasily. "I thought I heard a wagon, but I don't see any carriage lanterns out there, so I probably imagined it."

"Surely anyone driving a wagon in this storm would stop here for shelter until it passed," Helen said. "Unless it was Dabby and Uriah, trying to get home to feed their livestock."

I didn't mention the other thought that came to my mind. The unholy four were out there somewhere, and what better cover could they use for their illegal activities than a storm such as this?

"Do you want me to walk over to check on Uriah and Dabby?" I asked instead,

"In the morning," Helen said. "You'd drown out there if you tried to go in this storm."

So I settled back into my chair by the fire, and our big guard dog put his head on my knee, hoping for a scratch behind the ears.

Right after milking the next morning, I saddled my horse and rode out to Uriah's place. The world seemed fresh-washed and new as the sun rose over the chaos left behind by the storm. Tree limbs were down everywhere I looked, and rushing water created new rivers and ponds in the low-lying places among the farm fields. As I approached Uriah's property, I noticed something strange about the old deserted barn in the field. The big doors were wide open, and it looked as if something was dangling from the center beam. A moment later I heard Uriah "hallooing" from the house. He trotted out to greet me with Dobby limping behind. Uriah was beaming with pride.

"Henry, my boy Dabby here took care of those murdering thieves last night all by himself! What a triumph. We were just about to head into town to claim the reward when we saw you riding down the road. Come take a look!"

I tied my horse to the porch railing and followed father and son toward the old barn. As we walked, Uriah told me the whole story. It seems the wagon I heard last night had indeed contained the unholy four, intent on more robbery. But the storm was much worse than they had anticipated, and so they stopped by Uriah's house and asked for a place to spend the night. Dabby had showed them into the barn and then offered them a drink of root beer he had prepared specially for them.

"I recognized the men from the pictures on the Wanted posters," the amateur herbalist told me earnestly. "And I'd seen one of the men before. Longstreet was always following my friend Tessie around, and I think he was the one who k-killed her with a scarf." Dabby stared down at his clubfeet and wiped his eyes. "So I put poison in the root beer and watched them die. Then I put them there, where everyone can see."

He pointed through the open barn doors. I stopped in my tracks as my mind finally registered what was inside. Four corpses had been strung up along the center beam. They dangled grotesquely, swaying as the breeze whipped through the open door. The men's skin was pale and greenish, their faces twisted with horror and pain. Unseeing eyes were sunk deep within their sockets. The vile smell of vomit wafted through the barn, and my own stomach churned in response. It had obviously not been an easy death for the unholy four. My body went cold at the sight.

Somehow, I made it through the rest of the conversation and we parted ways—me to go home and report the news to Helen, Uriah and Dabby to collect the reward on the dead

ROOT BEER

thieves. I made it halfway to my house before I was forced to throw myself off the horse and vomit my breakfast into a water-filled ditch. I kept picturing Dabby offering poisoned root beer to the four thieves and then solemnly watching as they died in torment. It was a cold-blooded act for someone as innocent and kind as Dabby.

Long after the bodies were cut down and buried, the swaying figures of four thieves could still be seen at night, hanging from the center beam of the decrepit old barn. The phantoms didn't seem to bother Uriah or Dabby, but I stopped visiting their place after dark. And I never drank root beer again.

19

The French Paymaster

CANTON, CONNECTICUT

You couldn't grow up around Canton without hearing tales of the French Paymaster. On stormy nights, folks talked in hushed whispers over the cracker barrel at the mercantile or discussed the matter around the checkerboard by the pot-bellied stove at the tavern. Everyone told the same story.

The year was 1781 and America was in the midst of a revolution. One evening a French Paymaster stopped for the night at Dudley Case's Tavern on the old Albany Turnpike between Hartford and New York. His saddlebags clanked with gold coins when he laid them on the floor at his feet, for he was on his way to Saratoga with wages for the French soldiers stationed there. After eating a meal, the Paymaster retired to his room to sleep. He was never seen again. The innkeeper swore on a stack of Bibles that he had awakened the Frenchman at the appointed hour and sent him on his way. But the Paymaster never reached his destination. Man, horse, and gold vanished without a trace.

Shortly after his disappearance, a headless phantom appeared on the Albany Turnpike, rushing frantically each night in the direction of Saratoga, saddlebags clanking with gold. No one knew who killed the man, where his body lay buried, or what happened to his head, but all were agreed that this ghost was probably the restless spirit of the Paymaster trying to fulfill his duty by bringing the French soldiers their wages at Saratoga. A few months after the ghost appeared, some boys fishing on the creek found the remains of the man's horse and his empty saddlebags, but there was no trace of body or gold. So the disappearance remained a local mystery.

The phantom was nearly a hundred years old when I first heard the story as a schoolboy. The students all talked about a boy named Charlie who went down to the old Albany Turnpike near the creek late one night, hoping to see the ghost in action. The wind was howling and storm clouds were rising up over the horizon, blotting out the stars. Suddenly a bright light burst forth on the road above the creek. A horseman with no head galloped toward Charlie. Charlie screamed and scrambled to get out of the rider's way, but the phantom rode straight through his body and out the other side.

Charlie screamed in terror and ran home as fast as his trembling legs would carry him. When he arrived, his mother screamed too because Charlie's black hair had turned snow white in the instant the French Paymaster touched him. Oddly enough, there was no record of a boy named Charlie ever attending our school, but that didn't stop anyone from spreading the story around the playground.

I was just eighteen when the Civil War started, and I enlisted with my friends. Let me tell you, we saw so much horror on the battlefield that stories of the French Paymaster seemed tame in comparison. By the time we made it home to Canton— scarred physically and emotionally, but safe at last—we chuckled to think we were ever terrified by a ghost. My friends and I became regulars at the Hosford Stand, the new name given to Dudley Case's Tavern, where the French Paymaster spent his last evening.

In the days following the war, strangers traveling the old Albany Turnpike would occasionally burst through the front door, white and sweating, to report a ghostly encounter with a headless horseman. We'd buy each of the fellows a pint of ale and calm them down a bit. The strangers always rented a room for the night, unwilling to chance a second encounter with the French Paymaster.

About a year after I returned home, another ghostly victim came staggering through the door of Hosford Stand as the bartender was calling the last round. I recognized the man at once. His name was Geoffrey, and he had been in my regiment during the war.

"A ghost," Geoffrey gasped to the room at large. "A headless ghost! He ran me off the road and my horse bolted. I nearly lost my own head to a tree branch before I got him calmed down." He was trembling from head to toe and stood wringing his hands.

"Geoffrey, sit down," I called, leaving my spot by the fire to grab his arm. Geoffrey swayed as he tried to focus blurry eyes on me. I caught him before he fainted and pushed him into my vacated chair. After taking a few deep breaths, he looked up into my face and his eyes widened. "Able! Able, is that you? Oh, thank God. Able, I dropped my mother's locket back there. Remember the lucky locket that I carried through the war? A branch ripped it off my neck when my horse bolted off the road. You have to get it back for me!"

119

This was serious and I knew it. Geoffrey had survived both Antietam and Gettysburg wearing his mother's locket around his neck. If I didn't go right away and look for it, he'd probably head right back out on the old Albany Turnpike tonight to look for it and die from a heart attack if the French Paymaster was still lurking about.

The bartender appeared beside me with a glass of ale. He handed it to Geoffrey, who took several deep gulps. My comrade-in-arms was calming down, but not quickly. I exchanged glances with my local friends. "You fellows look after Geoffrey here," I said. "I'll go look for his locket."

"I ain't sure that's wise, Able," the bartender said. We'd known each other forever. In fact, he was the one who first told me about the ghost of the French Paymaster way back when.

"Geoffrey saved my life at Antietam," I said simply. And that was that.

My buddies rallied around Geoffrey, plying him with blankets and hot soup and more ale. I grabbed my coat with sweaty hands, put on my hat, and took a lantern from the rack. I'd faced down the Confederate army more than once. Surely I could face down a headless ghost. Poor choice of words, I thought as I slipped out the door. No face on a headless ghost.

Geoffrey's horse was tied to the rail and it looked wiped out. I took the poor critter to the barn and got it calmed down and settled. Then I set off to find that locket. Everyone knew the general vicinity of the ghost sightings, a little way up from the creek. If Geoffrey went off the road in the usual place, his locket was probably in the woods near the stream. It would be hard to see in the dark, but the moon was nearly full, so that would help some.

The wind whipped around my hair and howled down my collar. I shuddered, pretending I was just cold. Not an easy pretense in midsummer. I stomped my way toward the creek and found the place where the underbrush had been disturbed by Geoffrey's horse. I began combing the woods, searching for a gleam of metal among the bushes and brambles and tall grass. It was an exercise in futility, but I searched for more than an hour, until my lantern started to gutter. No locket. Geoffrey would be devastated.

Sadly, I pushed my way through the bushes and stepped back onto the road. And stopped dead in my tracks. A wave of cold air rushed over me, and all my hair stood on end as I beheld a dark figure sitting on a dark horse. The headless horseman glowed from within, his internal light overpowering the glow of the moon overhead. The trees around me lashed in a supernatural wind caused by the phantom's appearance. Flickering moon shadows danced over me and the French Paymaster.

I drew in a deep breath, wanting to run. But my legs felt stiff as boards. I couldn't move a muscle. Slowly, the headless phantom raised an arm and pointed into the shrubbery a few yards to my right. As if under a spell, my body instantly marched toward the spot where the phantom pointed without any input from my terrified brain. A foot from the road, a shimmering gold locket dangled from the limb of a tree. I reached up in awe and untangled it. As soon as the locket touched my hand, the spell released me and the ghost vanished.

"Th-thank you," I called into the darkness. Then I hurried back to the tavern to return the locket to its rightful owner.

A few years after my encounter with the French Paymaster, the Hosford Stand burned to the ground. I was part of the

THE FRENCH PAYMASTER

clean-up crew after the fire was extinguished. As we were digging out the rubble, I came across a skeleton buried in the floor, along with some ragged fragments of leather and bits of cloth that looked as if they might have been a Frenchman's uniform. There was no head attached to the skeleton. We found it a few feet away.

So the French Paymaster never left the inn, I mused, tenderly placing the bones in a casket. I bet it was the original innkeeper who killed him. Folks in Canton had often speculated on the source of the man's prosperity, especially during the lean times following the Revolutionary War. Here was one possible explanation. But we would never know for sure.

We buried the French Paymaster in the local cemetery, hoping this would put an end to his ghostly rides. But folks traveling the old Albany Turnpike at night sometimes still see the headless phantom frantically riding toward Saratoga, trying in vain to deliver the wages to the waiting French soldiers. He cannot rest until his task is complete.

20

The Séance

CHITTENDEN, VERMONT

My wife and I had never gone to a séance before, and I can't say I was all that keen to visit the famous spiritualists William and Horatio Eddy. I didn't believe in ghosts. But my wife lost her baby sister not too long ago under tragic circumstances and she was determined to speak to her one last time, if such a thing were possible. And all the reports about the Eddy brothers claimed this was not only possible, but probable if we attended a séance at their farmhouse in Chittenden. So early one August afternoon, I hitched the horses to the carriage, and my wife and I drove toward the Eddys' place.

The horses were well rested and made good time down the road, but it was a long drive nonetheless, which gave me time to reflect on what I'd heard about the Eddys. Apparently, their mediumistic talents manifested at birth. Invisible hands rocked their cradles. They played with unseen children and were removed from school after ghostly activities disrupted class whenever they were present. At first their father thought it was all hogwash and punished them whenever spirit activity disrupted daily life. Later he decided to take advantage of their gifts and toured the country showing off his ghost-haunted children. Large crowds gathered wherever they went, and their father went to great lengths to prove that his boys were not faking their trances and that the manifestation of the spirits was genuine.

When their father died in 1874, the Eddy brothers retired to their home in Chittenden and began holding nightly séances. Anyone was welcome to attend. Skeptics were encouraged to visit and test their powers. Visitors from all over the world paid ten dollars (what an expense!) to spend a week at the farm, and they had free run of the house and grounds.

Many newspaper reporters and spiritualist experts visited the Eddys—including the famous New York investigator Colonel Henry Steel Olcott—to try to prove that the brothers were frauds. They carefully inspected the house and grounds for secret passageways and hidden contraptions. They found nothing. They poked and pried at the roof, floor, and walls of the spirit closet where William and Horatio Eddy went into their nightly trances, but not one of them ever found a trapdoor, a secret entrance, or even a loose board that could rationalize a frame-up. And night after night, spirits of all shapes and sizes manifested themselves at the séances. Some of the phantoms were voices; some were wisps of light; and some were as solid as you and me, until they vanished before the eyes of their incredulous observers. The ghosts came in every color known to humankind and spoke in languages unknown to the Eddy brothers, but well known to their international clientele.

After reading about the Eddys in the newspaper, I made the mistake of showing the story to my wife. As soon as she learned that the Eddy brothers lived just an hour away from our Vermont home, she was determined to attend the very next séance. And so here we were, trotting down the long road to the Eddys' place on a glorious summer afternoon, hoping to see a ghost.

My primary role on this trip was support personnel and carriage driver, which was fine by me. I was looking forward to the visit, truth to tell. Being on the side of the skeptics, I planned to investigate the spirit closet and the séance room while my wife consulted with the mediums. Maybe I would be the one to debunk the Eddy mystique and solve the mystery of the myriad apparitions, where so many others had failed.

I was surprised when we reached our destination to discover that the Eddy place was just an unremarkable two-story farmhouse. I guess I was expecting a mysterious mansion of some kind. There were a few guests already in residence, with more expected after supper. We paid in advance for the privilege of dining with the family, and then my wife sat talking with Mary Eddy and some of the believers while the skeptic (meaning me) mounted the stairs to the room above the kitchen where the séance would be held.

The room was roughly circular and could hold up to a hundred people at a time. Wooden benches faced a platform with a small enclosed cabinet on it—the famed "spirit closet." I tapped every inch of that blasted cupboard, searching for a door or a crawl space or a hidden compartment. I couldn't find any possible way that an Eddy could slip out of that closet once it was locked and costume himself up as a ghost. Blast. I even got under the platform and tapped the floor underneath the cupboard. Still nothing. The walls of the séance room had no unusual thicknesses, not even around the fireplace. If the Eddy brothers were frauds, I couldn't see how they pulled it off. Maybe something would show up during the séance itself.

I'd just finished my investigations when we were all called to supper. Over the simple meal, my wife introduced me to the other guests. They were a varied lot. There was an Ohio farmer and his wife; an elderly couple from Germany; a sea captain from Connecticut; a honeymooning couple from French Canada; and a dark-haired man and his young daughter, who had just emigrated to New York from Japan. We managed to communicate across the various language barriers, all except the little girl who only spoke a word or two in English. But she smiled shyly at me when I smiled at her, and carefully accepted one of the toffees that I always kept in my waistcoat pocket as a treat for my own children.

While William Eddy finished washing the supper dishes, Horatio escorted us upstairs and Mary lit the lanterns. William arrived moments later and took center stage on the platform. I was expecting a speech or some dramatic utterance. But he simply said: "I am ready." Then he entered the spirit cabinet.

Silence fell over the assembly. I held my breath as anticipation built up. The air shimmered with the kind of energy usually felt just before a thunderstorm. I felt a buzzing in my ears and rubbed them in irritation. What was that annoying hum? I glanced along the row of spectators, wondering if one of them was the source of the noise. But everyone was silent, even the little girl sitting on her father's knee. No one moved. No throat vibrated.

Then the disembodied singing began. It sounded like a lullaby sung in a language I'd never heard. But someone recognized it. The little girl's eyes widened in amazement, and then she called out something in Japanese. At her words, a light appeared in front of the spirit cabinet and grew until it was the size and shape of a petite, smiling woman. The girl called out again and strained forward against her father's restraining hands. I think the apparition was her mother. Her father's eyes were wet with tears, and the spirit spoke gently to him in Japanese. The little girl broke in, babbling excitedly as the spirit drifted off the platform until it hovered in front of them. She reached out a hand and caressed the little girl's face. Then she faded away. Beside me, my wife wiped her eyes on a lace handkerchief. Silence fell once again.

The air in the room seemed colder than it had before the ghost's appearance. I glanced over at Horatio and Mary. They sat as still as the rest of us. I think they were in a light trance. Supporting William? Calling the spirits? Who knows.

A woman's voice cried suddenly: "Violet! Are you there?"

The Ohio woman jumped. "I'm here," she replied. A shimmering blue ball of light, more transparent than solid, bobbed at the edge of the platform.

"Where did you put my teeth, Violet? You said I'd be buried with my false teeth," the ball called irritably.

"I did bury you with your teeth, Granny," the woman protested.

"You buried me in my second-best pair," the blue ball howled. "My best pair is still in the top drawer of the armoire, underneath the lavender sachet. Promise me you'll put them in my coffin! Promise!"

The Ohio woman was shaking with nerves. "I promise, Granny! I promise."

Satisfied, the blue ball vanished with a pop like a cork coming out of a bottle.

I shuddered and grabbed my wife by the hand. I didn't like that second ghost.

The air lightened somewhat after the departure of the blue ball. It wasn't as cold, but the odd energy still circulated through the room. I glanced briefly down the row of faces, and when I looked back toward the platform, I gazed straight into the eyes of my sister-in-law.

"Mary," my wife breathed beside me. "Oh, Mary." She rose, trembling, and held out her arms. Mary stepped forward—as solid as she'd ever been in life—and hugged my wife close. My wife laid her head on Mary's shoulder and sobbed. "Do not worry, sister. I am fine. God is good. All is well," Mary whispered soothingly. She made eye contact and beckoned me closer with a nod. I stood on trembling legs and reached my wife just as Mary faded away. I wrapped my arms around my wife before she fell and led her back to the chair. Then I collapsed beside her, my body shaking so bad it was a wonder the chair didn't break.

As I sat breathing deeply in shock, a Frenchman spoke at length with his daughter and her new husband and then a big German ghost bellowed happily at his best friend and told jokes to make the man's pretty Frau laugh with delight.

I didn't laugh with her. I was sweating profusely and wanted to bolt from that circular room with its ghosts. I'd never wanted something so badly in all my life. It was too much. I was a skeptic. I'd come here hoping to prove the Eddys' phantoms were fake. But that had really been Mary. I recognized my sister-in-law's ghost as soon as I saw her. It made my mind shudder.

Beside me, my wife clutched my hand. She was still weeping quietly. I stared down at our joined fingers. Please let this German ghost be the last, I prayed. Please.

"Hello, Tom," a voice said directly in front of me. I caught my breath, still staring down at my fingers. I knew that voice. I knew it as well as I knew my own. I closed my eyes, fighting for control. I would not break down in front of these strangers. I would not.

"Hello, Father," I said when the urge to cry had passed. My father had died when I was fifteen.

I looked up from my hands and saw him sitting on the air in front of me, leaning back as if he reclined on his favorite couch.

"I see you married the girl next door," Father said conversationally. "Good man. Hello, Jillian."

"Hello, Father," my wife said softly. I glanced quickly at her. She was smiling through her tears.

"Your baby is here with me," my father said. "I was there when he passed, and God put him right into my arms."

An infant appeared in my father's arms, cooing and waving small hands. My little firstborn. My son who died when he was eight days old. He was dressed in the tiny blue outfit my wife sewed for him and wrapped in the soft blanket my mother knit to keep him warm. As soon as I saw my son, I lost it. Tears streamed down my checks as I stared at my baby. My little Freddy. He was happy and well and with my father. Thank you, God.

Father loosened one arm from around the baby and held something out toward me. "Catch," he said, and tossed it through the air. Reflexively I caught the small metal object, my eyes still fixed on my baby.

"Love you, boy. Take good care of your family," Father said. And the two ghosts vanished.

I slumped against my wife, sobbing like a small boy. She held me tight and we cried together.

Sometime later, Mary Eddy gently helped us to our feet and led us downstairs. Reflexively, I put the metal object into my waistcoat pocket with the toffee. I would examine it later.

The Eddy family generously offered us a bed for the night, gratis, since we'd had two traumatic experiences in a row. But I wanted to get away from that haunted farm. So William and Horatio helped me hitch up the horses, lit the carriage lanterns, and handed Jillian into the seat beside me. We drove through the darkness in silence. My head was empty of thought. It was too much to take in. I concentrated on driving down the rutted road in the light of the lantern while Jill cuddled next to me and went to sleep, spent by emotion.

The hour passed quickly. Soon I was driving into my own yard. My mother, who was watching our three children, saw us through the kitchen window and came out onto the porch as I stopped the carriage and helped Jillian down. The two women talked eagerly as I drove the carriage into the barn and unhitched the horses. They were still talking when I arrived in the kitchen.

Mother had been crying, but she beamed beatifically at me. "You saw your father," she cried. "And baby Freddy."

"Yes," I said, determined not to break down twice in one day.

"What was it Father gave you?" she asked.

I blinked in surprise. "I don't know. I didn't look. I was too busy watching Freddy."

I reached into my waistcoat pocket and dug among the toffee until my fingers closed around the metal object. I pulled it out. It was Father's wedding ring. It had been buried with him many years ago.

THE SÉANCE

Mother started crying again when she saw the ring. I rubbed the gold band bemusedly and looked inside at the inscription engraved on it: "Forever yours, Maryanne."

I placed the ring on my mother's finger and kissed her on the forehead for my father.

Were ghosts real? As real as my father's ring, I decided, and led my tired wife upstairs to bed.

PART TWO

Powers of Darkness and Light

21

The Man Who Made Weather

HALLOWELL, MAINE

Now, when you saw old Uncle Kaler puttering around among the roses in the garden at the back of his house, you would never have taken him for the local wizard. No sir. Uncle Kaler was small and wrinkled and bald. He lived all alone on Loudon Hill and he was always giving flowers to folk passing on their way to Cobbossee or the Hook. 'Course, many of the folk traveling that road were not really passing at all. Oh, they all had some trumped-up excuse for their journey, but they were really coming to see Uncle Kaler, wanting good luck charms, or love potions, or cattle cures.

But potions and amulets were just his sideline business; Uncle Kaler was best known for his ability to manipulate the weather. He could whistle up a whirlwind, start and stop a storm, make it snow in summer, or send a warm blast of air to heat the coldest day. People consulting Uncle Kaler for the first time were sometimes amused by the antics of the wrinkled, elfin man as he tested the wind with his finger or twirled his soup spoon around in the air. But when they got home, they would find their pond suddenly filled to the brim due to a cloudburst, or the ruined orchard at the back of their property cleared by a freak tornado, and they never laughed at Uncle Kaler again.

'Course, manipulating the weather is a tricky business, and sometimes it can get away from a body, even one as talented as Uncle Kaler. The incident I remember best came on a warm and misty summer evening a few years back. Uncle Kaler had spent the evening working among his roses, and as dusk fell he gathered an armload of yellow blossoms and brought them into the kitchen. As he was fetching out a vase for his treasures, he heard a horse speeding up the hill and stopping right outside his door.

Uncle Kaler opened the door. A youngish fellow appeared panting on his doorstep, holding a pretty young lady by the hand. Uncle Kaler recognized the young man at once, though he did not know the young lady. William had spent much of his time sailing the seas, and had done quite well for himself. His parents were very proud of their youngest boy, though some looked down upon him because his family came from poor farming stock.

"Are you Mr. Kaler?" William asked breathlessly.

"Yes, indeed," said Uncle Kaler heartily. "And I am at your service."

"Mr. Kaler, Elizabeth and I are on our way to Hallowell to be married. But her relatives don't approve of the match. Somehow they found out we were eloping tonight. You can hear them behind us!"

And indeed, Uncle Kaler could hear the sound of bloodhounds baying away down the river.

"Mr. Kaler, if you don't help us, they will murder us both. Please, sir. I've been saving up. I can offer you a hundred

Spanish millers for the worst weather you've got, and I will give you another hundred when we come back."

Without a word, Uncle Kaler disappeared into the house. He went to his old sea chest standing under the window and took out a leather bag. Going back to the door, he handed the bag to William and said: "Go back down the road and release the contents of this bag. Then throw the bag into the millstream. When you return, you will be able to continue your journey undisturbed."

William looked at the bag suspiciously, but did as he was told.

While Elizabeth gazed anxiously down the road after her bridegroom, Uncle Kaler went back into the kitchen to get some roses. Handing them to Elizabeth, he smiled shyly and said: "A wedding present from your good friend Uncle Kaler."

Elizabeth blushed happily and thanked him.

A moment later, William rode back up the road. "I've done it," he said. "But nothing happened. If you've played us false, Mr. Kaler . . ."

He tried to look threatening but only managed to look frightened. Uncle Kaler just smiled.

"Listen," he said.

There came a low grumble of thunder from the southwest. It increased in volume, and the wind rose sharply and began to pummel the tops of the trees.

"Is it a cyclone?" Elizabeth squeaked in terror.

"Just a cloudburst," Uncle Kaler said soothingly. "In about five minutes not one of those hounds will be able to find you. No, no, keep your money," he added as William tried to press the Spanish millers on him. "Buy a pretty house for your new wife."

THE MAN WHO MADE WEATHER

Elizabeth blushed at the word wife and then boldly kissed Uncle Kaler's cheek. They mounted the horse, and Uncle Kaler called: "Good luck to you, from a man who can make his own luck."

They rode quickly toward Hallowell through the gathering storm. The thunder was roaring almost continuously now, and lightning lit up the sky as a torrent of rain suddenly drenched Uncle Kaler where he stood by the garden gate.

"Hmm," he said, waving his hand. The rain parted and fell on either side of him. "I think I may have made that bag a tad bit too strong. Well, at least it will give those young folk a chance. It would never do for them to get caught."

He shook himself and was instantly dry. Then he walked up the path to the door, the rain falling away before it reached him and then pouring back into the gap when he had passed.

"Perhaps one teaspoon less of tansy," he muttered, closing his door against the raging torrent. Uncle Kaler opened the door again and told the rain: "You stay away from my roses!" The rain around the house stopped instantly. Nodding his approval, he shut the door and went to bed. All around Hallowell and the surrounding towns, a great storm raged all night long, except over Uncle Kaler's garden.

The next morning dawned bright and clear. Uncle Kaler whistled cheerfully as he went out into his garden. But a strange sound met his ears. Above the chirping of the birds came the rushing sound of water running through a gorge. The millstream had never sounded like that before, even when it flooded. Going to investigate, Uncle Kaler found that the millstream had been replaced by a raging torrent coursing through a deep gorge.

It was filled with uprooted trees and brush. The mill itself was completely gone.

Following this new landscape, Uncle Kaler soon spotted the huge boulder that was once part of the foundation of the mill. It had been swept clean into the river and would create a nasty obstacle in the future to anyone traveling upon it. A long muddy point stretched out into the river from the mouth of the brook. The grindstone from the mill was nowhere to be seen.

"Definitely too much tansy," said Uncle Kaler. Then he shrugged and went home to his roses.

22

The Bridge

MONTPELIER, VERMONT

The wind was whipping the rain right into his eyes. Charlie Stevens brushed the water off his face and hunched down in the saddle, trying to ignore his discomfort. His horse was plodding slowly down the dark, sodden road, splashing through puddles and occasionally snorting his negative opinion of the weather. The night was so dark and chilly that Charlie could barely see. If it hadn't been for his horse, he would have wandered off the road.

"What a horrible night," Charlie said to his horse, Bo. Bo shook his head at the sound of his master's voice. The sound of the rattling bit was the most cheerful thing Charlie had heard all night. They both continued on in gloomy silence. The wind whistled in Charlie's ears and he wished fervently for his hat, which he had inadvertently left at the home of the friend whom he had been visiting. He could hear the sound of the Winooski River, much swollen by a steady week of rain, roaring somewhere ahead. At least he was getting close to home. Less than an hour's ride and he would be able to dry off by the fire and tell his wife all the news from their friends.

Another miserable fifteen minutes in pitch darkness brought them to the edge of the river. Charlie had to strain his eyes to make out the outline of the bridge. The river sounded unusually loud, but he put it down to the rain.

"We're almost home," Charlie said to Bo. Bo did not seem to be attending him. The horse had stopped on the bank and seemed to be studying the bridge.

"Get up, Bo. Let's go home," Charlie said, nudging the horse lightly to get his attention.

Bo shook his head again, giving another snort of distress. He bunched his muscles and then stepped carefully onto the bridge. Charlie frowned a bit. Crossing the bridge had never bothered Bo before. The sound of the raging river must be making the poor horse nervous, he decided. The rain and the wind picked up at this juncture, and Charlie huddled deeper into his coat, too miserable to ponder the small mystery any further. He just let Bo carry him across as he dreamed of hearth and home.

Another ten minutes found Charlie unsaddling Bo and putting him in the warm barn with some food. Bo whickered happily and nibbled Charlie's wet hair. Charlie patted him absently and hurried into his warm house. It was silent. Everyone had gone to bed. But his wife, Melissa, must have been listening for him, because she came into the room and greeted him with a kiss. She fussed over his wet clothes, and within a few minutes Charlie was in a warm dressing gown and sipping tea in front of the fire.

"Which way did you come?" his wife asked presently, sitting down across from him with her own cup.

"The same way I went, of course," Charlie said absently, a bit puzzled by the question.

"Charlie, don't tease," she rebuked him gently. "The bridge was stripped of all its planks yesterday. Don't you remember me telling you that they were going to replank it and add some new string pieces?"

"They must have delayed the project," Charlie said. "I came across the bridge, same as always."

"Charles Stevens, don't you fib to me!" Melissa cried. "Mrs. Smith's boy was helping out at the bridge yesterday, and he told her there was not a plank left in place. And the river is too high for you to ford right now. Honestly, it's late, and I've had a hard day. I am not in the mood for your jokes."

"I'm not joking," protested Charlie, feeling hard done by. "The boy must have been talking about another bridge."

"I am going to bed," said Melissa, slamming her cup down on the side table. She marched away, leaving Charlie to shake his head in wonder over the silliness of women.

Melissa was still sore the next morning, and Charlie ate his breakfast in silence. Their neighbor Mr. Parker knocked on the kitchen door while Charlie was finishing his food.

"'Morning, Charlie. Glad you're back," he said, nodding to Melissa. "I'm afraid I need to borrow some of your tools."

"Charlie claims he came over the bridge last night on his way home," Melissa said sourly. "Honestly, sometimes I can't stand his silly jokes."

"How'd you do it, man? Fly?" asked Mr. Parker jovially. "I heard tell they stripped the planks clean off the bridge just the other day."

THE BRIDGE

"I'm telling you, the bridge was fine!" Charlie was getting upset. "Come on and I'll show you. It was muddy enough last night. Bo's hoofprints will tell the true story."

So the three of them walked to the bridge. The river was still roaring in its banks, but the sun was shining and the birds were chirruping merrily. Charlie would have enjoyed the walk if it hadn't been for the ribbing he was getting from Mr. Parker. When they turned the corner and saw the bridge, Charlie stopped. Above the raging river was the naked frame of the bridge, the planking all stripped away.

"Oh my Lord," Charlie gasped. The color drained from his face as the impact of this discovery penetrated his mind. He must have crossed the river on one of the string pieces! Charlie fainted dead away.

It took a few minutes for Melissa and Mr. Parker to rouse him. Charlie refused to even look at the bridge, so Mr. Parker finally went over to search for Bo's hoofprints. He came back after a while, shaking his head.

"Somebody crossed that bridge last night," he said soberly. "There are muddy hoofprints all along the broadest of the string pieces."

Melissa turned pale. "Charlie, you might have been killed," she gasped.

"You don't have to tell me," Charlie muttered, trying to still his shaking hands.

"It's a miracle you are still alive," said Mr. Parker soberly. "There must have been an angel guiding your horse."

"Thank you, God," Melissa whispered, hugging her trembling husband.

Mr. Parker crossed himself and said: "Amen."

23

The Witch-Sheep

NARRAGANSETT, RHODE ISLAND

Old Benny Nicols lay abed on Christmas morning in the year of 1811, unable to sleep. The room was gray with the predawn light, and Benny tossed and turned, wondering why he couldn't sleep. Much to his resentment, his wife Debby never stirred. Finally Benny lit a candle and went to look at the clock on the fireplace mantel. The hands pointed to nine o'clock. Shivering with the cold, Benny stared at it incredulously and then went to the window. At once he saw that a huge fall of snow had covered the window, thus producing the illusion of night.

"Debby," he shouted to his wife. "Debby, it's nine o'clock and we've jest had the worst snowstorm I ever seen. Debby, my new sheep will be drowned for sure!"

Debby sprang out of the bed just as the mantel clock struck nine, and hurried down to start breakfast. Old Benny followed at her heels. Benny was the shepherd for a large Narragansett farm, and he knew full well the dangers of such a blizzard. He had once tried to rescue a large flock of sheep that were cringing and hiding themselves one behind another near the open shore. In their frantic efforts to shelter from the fierce beating of the storm, they inadvertently backed themselves into the sea; most of the flock were lost, despite Benny's most valiant efforts.

Benny was all for digging himself out of the house immediately, but Debby made him put on some clothes, and she even forced him to wear his Sunday longboots. Benny put up a bit of a struggle about the boots, him being a prudent man and wanting to get another ten years of wear out of them. But Debby wouldn't let him out of doors without those boots, so he gave in.

Benny quickly dug a path upward through the snow until he reached the surface. There he saw at once that the wind had blown the snow away from the water, so none of the flock would have been drowned. He set off over the deep snow, looking for his flock. He noticed a suspicious-looking drift by one of the hayricks and soon had dug out the sheep buried beneath it. This accounted for about half the flock. Searching farther, he found the remainder buried beside a high stone wall. By lunchtime Benny had rescued all but one of the flock, a pretty little creeper ewe who was the most valued of all.

Benny was upset that he had lost his ewe, though justly proud that he had managed to rescue his flock. Many others had lost most of their livestock, and some their lives, in the unexpected blizzard. Still, Benny repeatedly told Debby that he might have found the ewe if he hadn't slept so late on Christmas morning. "I wouldn't have minded spoilin' my Sunday boots if I'd found the creeper, Debby," he said mournfully.

It was three weeks later, while he was checking a hayrick about a mile from his home, that Benny saw a breathing hole in the snow by the rick. He knew at once that a living animal must be trapped under the snow, so he broke away the crust of ice.

And there was a poor, starving creature that looked so unlike a sheep it took Benny a moment to recognize the creeper ewe. In her desperation to survive, the hungry creeper had eaten every blessed fiber of her wool within reach of her mouth. She lay bare and trembling in the snow gazing up at Benny, too weak to bleat. Benny wrapped her gently in his cloak and took her home to Debby.

Debby worked over the poor creeper for hours, offering her small amounts of warm milk until the ewe was able to digest ordinary food. In a week the little ewe had regained her health and was poking her little black muzzle everywhere it didn't belong, much to Debby's chagrin. But they couldn't put her outside in the snow while she was shorn. So Debby decided to make her a false fleece that would keep her warm until spring.

Debby took an old blue coat that used to belong to her son and cut the sleeves to just the right length to fit the front legs of the little ewe —whom she had named Nanny. At the waist of the blue coat, she attached two sleeves from an old red flannel shirt. Debby pulled the jacket up over Nanny's little legs and buttoned the large brass buttons along her back. Nanny was quite taken with her new garb and pranced around the house, looking like an overgrown organ-grinder's monkey.

When old Benny carried her out to the fenced-in yard where the flock were gathered, Nanny gave a delighted bleat and wriggled out of his arms, eager to be among her companions again. To a sheep, the rest of the flock bolted around and around the yard, crowding against the fence, running from side to side and bleating in terror at the sight of the terrible beast trotting among them. They created such a ruckus that Benny was forced to capture Nanny and carry the reluctant ewe back into the house.

As night fell, Benny took Nanny back out to the yard, hoping that in the dim light the other sheep would grow used to her jacket and allow her to graze with them. Then he hurried back inside, just in time to greet two of his oldest friends, who had come for a visit.

The three old men sat by the large fireplace, nursing drinks and watching the fire crackle as Debby rubbed and rubbed tallow into the poor, abused Sunday longboots. They were all startled by a sudden terrible wailing, and the door to the kitchen was thrust open by Tuggie Bannocks, who stumbled in and dropped breathlessly into a chair near the fire. Rocking back and forth, Tuggie cried hysterically: "Tanks be to God! Tanks be to God!"

Tuggie Bannocks was a freed slave who lived on a small farm near the Petaquamscut River. She and Debby made soap together every year, and the combination of Tuggie's strong arms and her voodoo spells always caused Debby's soap to turn out exactly right. Tuggie occasionally bought wool from old Benny in the winter months, so her visit to the farm was no surprise, though the Nicolses and their guests could not understand what had caused her distress.

"Tuggie!" Debby cried, rushing to the old woman, pulling off her mittens, and rubbing the thin hands with her own. Benny hurried to close the door against the cold, wondering how he could help. Then he remembered his mother repeating the old adage that burned feathers were supposed to revive a faint. He thrust the turkey feather duster into the fire and stuck the smoking mess under Tuggie's nose. Acrid smoke filled the room and everyone began coughing and choking until Debby grabbed the duster away from Benny and doused it with water.

"Heaven ha' mercy, I ain't dead yet, Benny Nicols," gasped Tuggie. "But," she added in a fainter voice, "I'se expect I soon will be." She eyed the mugs of beer on the table. Benny rushed to get her one, adding a dash of Jamaican rum and heating the whole thing with a red-hot loggerhead. Tuggie accepted the drink with alacrity and, when she finished it, she was ready to tell her story.

"Well, I told ya a few weeks back, Miz Nicols, that I am being witch-rid by ol' Mum Amey. See, I was tryin' to work a charm on her first, not to hurt her o' course, I jest wanted to bother her a bit. Well, I had the spell boilin' away in the kettle when in she walks without knockin' and asks me what I'm cookin'. I don't want her to know I'm cookin' up a spell to put on her, so I says I'm makin' glue and I takes the pot off the fire. 'Course, now me spell is ruined, and Mum Amey knows it. And ever since that day I been witch-rid."

Tuggie paused, waiting for a response from her audience. Benny and his old cronies nodded solemnly, and Debby gave a horrified gasp. Satisfied, Tuggie pointed dramatically to her mouth. "See these marks on the corner of me mouth?" she said.

Debby nodded eagerly, hanging on her every word.

"Them marks are on account of Mum Amey's been ridin' me in my sleep all over Ridge Hill and Boston Neck. I wake up so tired most mornings that I can hardly work. And I been pinched in the night and my hair's been pulled. Even me butter won't come right 'less I drop a hot horseshoe into the cream to drive Mum Amey out of it.

"So I decides to lay a trap fer her, to see if she's really a witch. I watch fer Mum Amey till she walks toward me down the road. Then I drops a silver sixpence in her path. Well, Miz Nicols, before she gets to it, Mum Amey turns and goes back the way she came. Proof 'nuff, says I, 'cause everyone knows a witch can't step over silver."

"No indeed," Debby said, and the men nodded their agreement.

"Well, Benny Nicols," Tuggie cried, flinging her free arm wide, "I jest seen that ol' witch Mum Amey a-ridin' and a-chasin' yer sheep out there in the moonlight. As sure as yer born, you'll find them all dead come the morning."

Benny was thunderstruck. He wanted to run out and save his sheep, but he was too superstitious to face a witch like Mum Amey.

"What did she look like, Tuggie?" Debby asked in a whisper. "What was she doin' out there?"

"Well, Miz Nicols, witches don't never take their true form when they goes out on a witches' Sabbath. Mum Amey was long and low to the ground, sort of like a snake. She was a-runnin' and a-springin' and a-chasin' them poor sheep all 'round the yard. They's in quite a panic. She was wearin' her old red-and-blue Injun blanket, that's how I knowed her. And she had sparklin' gold dollars all down her back—the wages of the Devil fer sure. And she were lashin' her long black tail as if she were the Devil hisself."

"It sounds jest like the Devil," cried Debby excitedly, "or maybe the creeper."

Benny struck his forehead with his palm and burst out laughing. He had forgotten all about little Nanny in her brightly

THE WITCH-SHEEP

colored jacket. Gasping with merriment, he explained to his cronies that the "witch" was really his creeper sheep in her false fleece. He offered to go alone to face the "Devil" in the field, and bring her in to prove it.

Tuggie was insulted. She jumped up and shook her fist angrily at Benny, ignoring Debby's placating remarks that Benny was probably wrong and it was Mum Amey out in the field. Then Tuggie stopped her ranting, and a malicious smile lit up her face. She shook Debby's hand off her sleeve, gathered up her mittens, and marched to the door. They could hear her muttering to herself as she stomped away: "Best to stop such outrageous goin's-on right now. Dressin' sheep up like they was a witch and scarin' a poor ol' woman. But Tuggie Bannocks knows how to stir up a spell or two sose they won't laugh at witches no more."

"Benny Nicols, now look what you've done," Debby said severely. Benny just laughed at Tuggie's threats.

But as the days passed, Debby and Benny knew that Tuggie really had witched them. Their cakes and roasts always burned no matter how carefully they were tended, the chimney spat smoke and soot at them, and they could hear Tuggie dancing on the roof and shouting down the chimney at them when the wind grew wild. She even be-spelled the old ram, who never grew accustomed to Nanny's new outfit, though the other sheep accepted her. The old ram grew thin and faded, and Benny was afraid he would lose the ram all together. He and Debby went so far as to purchase a few charms from Mum Amey, but nothing seemed to work.

Finally, after all the sheep were sheared and Nanny was released from her coat, the ram ceased to be witch-rid, and with the false fleece discarded, Tuggie's spell was worked out at last.

For years afterward people around about Narragansett liked to tell the story of Tuggie Bannocks and the false fleece. Nanny and her descendants became famous from Point Judith to Pottawomat, and all the creepers sold throughout Narragansett ever after went by the name of witch-sheep.

24

The Black Dog of Hanging Hills

MERIDEN, CONNECTICUT

Justin stepped out of the front door of his Meriden hotel and stretched. He had arrived a day early for the hiking vacation he was taking with his best friend, Tom. The drive had been a long one, and he felt the need to stretch his legs while there was still some afternoon left. He didn't want to get back into the car, but he was eager to get his first glimpse of Hubbard Park.

When Tom had first recommended hiking the Hanging Hills in Connecticut, Justin had been skeptical. Connecticut was not the first place that had come to his mind when considering a vacation. But as usual, Tom had been right. It was beautiful here, despite the rain. Tom was enthusiastic about hiking the Metacomet Trail, part of which went through Hubbard Park, where there was a stone observation tower on East Peak called Castle Crag. Then the trail meandered over West Peak, 1,024 feet above sea level.

"From Castle Crag," Tom had said, "you can see the Sleeping Giant Mountain Range to the south, and on a clear day you can catch a glimpse of Long Island Sound. To the north you can see all the way to the foothills of the Berkshires!"

I won't go too far, Justin said to himself as he pulled into the parking lot. *Just get a bit of a preview.*

If the gorgeous landscapes he had seen as he traveled along I-691 were any indication, then he and Tom were in for a real treat the next day when they hiked the Metacomet.

Justin found his way easily to the blue-blazed trail. The rain was a bit heavier now, and no one was in sight. He was quite high on the mountain when he heard barking. He looked around him and saw a medium-size black dog with great big brown eyes and a long silky tail trotting up the path toward him.

"Well, where did you come from?" Justin asked. The dog pranced about, his whole back end wagging with his tail.

"Would you like to take a walk?" Justin asked him. The dog barked excitedly and rushed ahead a few yards. Then he paused and looked back at Justin expectantly. Justin laughed. His parents had two black Labradors back at home. He had seen that look before.

"I'm coming!" he said, and hurried after the dog.

They hiked the mountain trails for another half hour before Justin reluctantly turned back toward town.

"You must be getting hungry, too," he said to his canine companion. The dog wagged his tail enthusiastically. They proceeded back down the trail they had just climbed. But when Justin emerged onto the road, the dog was gone. He shrugged philosophically. After all, he couldn't take the dog home with him.

Realizing that he was soaked to the skin by the persistent drizzle, Justin hurried back to the inn to take a hot shower and change.

He dined that night at the inn restaurant. After enjoying a steak dinner, Justin lingered at the table, sipping his coffee

THE BLACK DOG OF HANGING HILLS

and reviewing the day. It had been an excellent—if short—hike. When Tom arrived in the morning, they would hike all the way over West Peak.

"Did you have a nice hike?" asked the pretty blond waitress, coming over to refill his cup.

"Yes, indeed. I had some unexpected company," he said with a smile.

"Really? I thought you were the only one crazy enough to go hiking in the rain," she teased.

"It was a black dog," he said. "Cute fellow. Followed me all the way up the mountain and down again."

He looked up from his coffee to see that the waitress's face had gone pale.

"A black dog?" she asked. "That's not good."

"Why not?"

"We have a saying around here," she replied. "'And if a man shall meet the Black Dog once, it shall be for joy; and if twice, it shall be for sorrow; and the third time, he shall die.'"

He laughed. "That's just superstition."

She did not laugh with him.

"That's what a man named Mr. Pynchon said, back in the early 1900s," she said. "He saw the black dog twice. The second time he saw the dog, the friend he was climbing with fell to his death. And later, Mr. Pynchon decided to climb the same mountain, and he died, too. Everyone here believes he saw the dog just before he fell."

"Nonsense. That was years ago. This dog was just a cute stray," Justin said uneasily.

She shrugged. "I'd be careful if I were you." She then took the coffeepot over to her other customers.

Tom arrived early the next morning. When Justin told him about the black dog, he chuckled. "I should have warned you about the legend. Are you sure you want to go back up the mountain today?"

"Oh please," Justin said. They both laughed. Tom hurried into the inn with his luggage. As soon as Tom had settled into his room, they set out on their hike.

The day was perfect and the scenery was beautiful. Justin kept taking big breaths of the clean air. The narrow trail they followed twisted up and up. There were wildflowers everywhere. Justin saw bloodroot, trillium, and Dutchman's breeches. Now that the rain had cleared, he could better appreciate the splendid views.

"See, isn't this better than flying all the way to Colorado?" Tom called.

"It's not bad," Justin replied.

They stopped for a few minutes to admire the view from Castle Crag before they continued onward and up the steep path of West Peak. Suddenly Justin heard a familiar bark. He looked up. Farther up the steep trail stood the black dog, plumed tail waving. He looked deep into the friendly brown eyes as he called back to Tom: "There's the dog."

Justin's smile faded suddenly. The dog's eyes had begun to glow with a red light. A shudder of alarm went through his body, just before his foot slipped on the muddy trail. He plunged down the side of the mountain, desperately grabbing at rocks, trying to halt his descent. It seemed to take forever for him to stop sliding. There was a stabbing pain in his leg. When he looked at it, his head swimming, he saw that it was bent at an odd angle. He heard Tom yelling in panic just before he fainted.

They had to send in a mountain rescue team to get him off West Peak. At the hospital the doctor told Justin that his leg was broken in two places.

"I know that path," the doctor continued. "That was a nasty place to take a fall. You're very lucky to get away with only a broken leg."

Then the doctor let Tom come in.

"You know, that was a very strange fall," said Tom uneasily. "You don't really think it had anything to do with that black dog?"

Justin looked down at the cast that extended all the way up to his hip. "I don't know. But I don't really want to find out. Next time, let's go to Colorado."

Tom agreed.

25

Old Trickey

Now, mind you, I cannot prove that Trickey was the meanest, the orneriest, and the roughest fisherman who ever lived and worked in Maine. But if it wasn't him, well, then he came pretty darned close.

Trickey lived at the mouth of the York River, near Kittery. No one associated with him if they could help it, for he was malevolent, wicked, and prickly to boot. He had to keep his fish prices at rock bottom just to get anyone to buy from him. Not, as the wags of Kittery said, that fishing was how he *really* made a living.

No one in Kittery would have been surprised if they had known, when he died, that Old Trickey was turned over to the Devil himself on account of all his misdeeds.

"Well now, Trickey," said the Devil, said he, "it seems like you've managed to wound and offend jest about everybody living in and around Kittery. Tut, tut, we have been naughty."

"Not me fault," Trickey grumbled. "They jest dint understand me." A typical complaint that the people of Kittery could all parrot, and the wags at the tavern often did.

"Well, Trickey, this here record says it was your fault," said the Devil, said he. "I think you're gonna have to hang around this harbor for a long time, Trickey. Seems like I need someone to bind sand, Trickey. Bind it and haul it 'round this here harbor. The sand's lookin' a bit thin over there. It's gonna take a lotta sand, Trickey, before this record's paid!"

"Not me fault," Trickey whined. "Not me fault. They jest dint understand me."

"Oh, I think they understood you jest fine," said the Devil. "Off you go, then."

And the Devil set Trickey to bindin' and haulin' sand with a rope. Old Trickey cursed, and fumed, and fretted, but he was tied to the harbor, and he had to bind the sand with a rope and haul it hither and thither at the Devil's bidding.

Now the Devil, he liked to play games with Old Trickey. Sometimes, jest when Trickey got a load of sand set jest so, the Devil would send a wind in and blow the sand away, jest so Trickey would be forced to bind it up again. This enraged Trickey, and he would fume and curse so loud the people 'round the harbor would shake their heads to hear him.

But when a storm began to gather, then the harbor folk would hear Old Trickey at his worst. As the wind and the rain blew ashore, whippin' up the waves, the wraith of Old Trickey would fly shriekin' over the land. "More rope, more rope," he cried. "More sand, more sand." Old Trickey would bind sand in a fury and then, hauling it to the shore, dump it atop the dunes, then scrape it out and throw it back into the waves.

After many years had passed, Old Trickey got fed up with the Devil's tricks. He gathered many lengths of rope and bound sand until he had a veritable mountain. Then he waited for

OLD TRICKEY

a giant gale to strike shore. When he saw the storm comin', Old Trickey let out such a shriek of rage that the people of the harbor prayed to the good Lord to spare them.

Then, as dusk fell and the storm gathered in strength, Old Trickey came roarin' inland. The bravest of the harbor folk watched Old Trickey growing larger and larger as he came, haulin' his mountain of sand behind him. But even the bravest hid their eyes as Old Trickey blew across the cottages and cabins, strewing sand everywhere as he howled his challenge to the Devil. The sand dunes shifted, the storm raged, and Old Trickey met the Devil in midair and wrestled with him over the harbor where he had labored so long.

Old Trickey's howlin' and shriekin' continued all night long as he grappled with the Devil at the height of the storm. Meanwhile, the fierce wind and rain were whipping the mountain of sand hither and thither, pelting the homes of the harbor folk, shifting old sand dunes, and creating new ones. But toward dawn all went silent. When the harbor folk ventured out of doors the next morning, the landscape was completely new. The sands had shifted and many a garden was now buried under Old Trickey's load. The atmosphere above the harbor was tremulous, and folk knew that Old Trickey was still wrestlin' with the Devil.

But a new breeze sprang up as they watched. It blew away the clouds and heartened the harbor folk so much that they began clearing away all the storm debris and Old Trickey's sand. As they worked, they heard a sudden boom from the surf. The Devil had thrown Old Trickey down into the harbor. On the breeze, the breaking waves seemed to mutter: *Not me fault. They jest dint understand me.*

So Old Trickey went back to his work, grumbling and complaining and cursing his fate. But bindin' and haulin' sand was his doom and everyone, even Old Trickey, knew the Devil would never be satisfied with his labors.

Sometimes, though, Old Trickey still gets fed up with the Devil's tricks. When he does, Old Trickey the sandman rises up during the next mighty gale and wrestles with the Devil till mornin'.

26

Mary's Flower

PROVINCETOWN, MASSACHUSETTS

She waited patiently, day after day, for her husband to return from fishing. They lived in a deserted shack in the place called Helltown. She kept the shack immaculately clean, and was very proud of her small family. The baby was well behaved, and would entertain himself for hours. Once the cooking and cleaning were done for the day, she had nothing to do except walk on the sand dunes with him, watching for her husband. Sometimes she would sit on the gray moss for hours with the little boy on her lap, watching the endless motion of the sea. She did not know much English yet, and her neighbors did not speak Portuguese, so she had no female companionship to while away the long hours.

But still her husband did not come. She worried now that something had happened to his small sailing dory. Or perhaps there were no fish. Each morning she would measure out the flour to bake a loaf of bread. At first there had been fish and vegetables to eat with the bread, and milk for the baby. But now there was only bread, and soon there would be nothing at all. That morning, as she measured out the last of the flour, she prayed to the Virgin Mary for a sign. Should she stay here where her husband could find her, or would the threat of starvation force her to leave her small home to seek help from strangers who could not speak her language? If her husband returned while they were away, he would not know where to find them and could not ask any of the neighbors, for his English was little better than hers.

She sat on the dunes, praying and wishing for her husband to come home. Storm clouds were gathering in the sky, and finally she swept the baby up into her arms and went back to the shack to stoke up the fire and warm the last of the bread for their dinner.

The storm came shrieking down upon their small home, as she rocked the boy in his cradle. She had saved a few slices of bread for their breakfast, though it meant going to bed hungry. She listened to the sound of the rain beating on the roof while tears rolled down her cheeks. Where was he? Why did he not come home?

A knock sounded on the door. She sat up, startled, brushing the tears from her cheeks. For a moment, her heart leapt. But she knew it could not be her husband, for he would not knock on the door of his own house. Still, who would be out on a night such as this? She hastened to open the door.

A small woman carrying a baby wrapped in a shawl stood shivering in the rain. "Please," the woman said in Portuguese, "may I stay here until the storm ceases?"

She drew the stranger in at once, exclaiming over her wet clothes and putting her in the best chair by the fire. She gave the woman the one blanket from the bed to warm herself and her baby, offered the woman the last of her bread to eat, and used the last bit of coffee to give her a warm drink. Then she tucked

MARY'S FLOWER

the woman and the baby into the bed and slept on the floor next to her baby's cradle.

The storm ceased during the night, and the day dawned clear and beautiful. The stranger gravely thanked her and said good-bye. She watched as the woman walked away across the gray moss. Then she blinked and rubbed her eyes. Under the woman's feet, the gray moss suddenly blossomed with beautiful yellow flowers. Above the woman's head, she could see a shining halo. As the yellow flowers spread across the dunes, she put her hands to her face and wept for joy. She had been visited by the Blessed Virgin Mary. This was the sign she had prayed for.

She found a loaf of bread and a pound of coffee on the table when she went into the house to check on the baby. Around noon she heard her name joyously shouted from the path outside the shack. She ran out the door with her baby, across the flowering moss, and was swept into her husband's arms.

To this day the Portuguese still call the yellow flower "Mary's flower."

27

The Fatal Glass Eye

SALEM, MASSACHUSETTS

My friend Liverpool Jarge was a small man, wiry and tough, but soft-spoken. He had only one eye, on account of the other one being knocked out by a belaying pin. I met Jarge in London when we both took work on a ship heading for the West Indies. My homeport was Salem, Massachusetts, in those days, and Jarge was happy to meet another fellow from Massachusetts. Although he was now a Liverpudlian, Jarge had been born in Massachusetts, and he remembered his roots. He often said to me, "Danny, we Yanks should stick together." Which was fine by me.

Now, Liverpool Jarge was covered from head to toe with tattoos. Used to be a hobby of his, to get a tattoo at every new port. While the other sailors went out drinking, Jarge was having birds and women and snakes and such tattooed all over him. He even had a crucifix between his shoulders to keep off the Devil.

When Jarge got down to his last white spot, he cried like a baby. He wanted something special for his last tattoo. Spent days discussing it with me, until finally he settled on an evil eye. We had to climb up three stories to a back room in Whitechapel to get Jarge that evil eye.

While the tattoo professor worked, we got to talking about eyes in general and glass eyes in particular. When Jarge's tattoo was finished, the tattoo professor took us downstairs to the glassblower's shop to look at the glass eyes the man had for sale.

Now, this glassblower was a real artist. His shop was full of spun-glass ships, birds, castles, and more. One shelf was dedicated to glass eyes. Fanciest things you ever did see, with stars and pretty stripes and more colors than any real eyes could ever have. Jarge was fascinated with those glass eyes.

Jarge's one real eye was a dull brown color, and his glass eye, the one he got in 'Frisco, was an ugly shade of blue. When this artist fellow offered to make Jarge a beautiful red eye with a white star in the middle (price, one pound), Jarge paid up at once. He was tickled pink with the idea. The very next day Jarge was back in the shop ordering two more glass eyes—one blue eye with a white snake, and one green eye with a yellow cross. Seems my friend had found himself a new hobby.

Well, the years passed and I sailed 'round the world a coupla times before I met Liverpool Jarge again. I had just got into London off a ship outta Boston, and Jarge had just come in from New York. We met accidentally on the dock, and he immediately took me 'round to his ship to see his collection of glass eyes. He'd got two or three each time he went ashore, and now had nearly twenty of 'em. Jarge claimed he was the pride of the forecastle on every ship he sailed on, and I believed him.

I went with Jarge when he placed his next order. Seemed to me that the novelty of collecting glass eyes had worn off, Jarge was that hard to please. Finally I kidded Jarge that he should get an evil eye, since the one on his belly was no good 'cause it was hidden by his shirt. Right away the glassblower said he could make a jolly good evil eye, and he'd make it hollow so it could be filled with deadly poison, in case Jarge ever came to be captured by cannibals and needed a quick out, so to speak. Jarge was as pleased as Punch, sayin' to me that a man never knew when he might get to the place where he'd want to commit suicide, and what could be easier than to pop the eye into his mouth and bite down?

Well, me and Jarge signed onto the same ship, the *Dunreagh Castle*, which was bound for Australia. Jarge's new eye was delivered the day before we set sail. And what a creepy eye it was, too—the perfect evil eye. It was made up of rings of color that narrowed into a single red spot. If you looked at it just right, the colors ran together and the red spot popped out and would scare the life outta you. It was hollow, too, like the man promised, and filled with a white liquid, sealed in by the thinnest glaze of glass. Jarge declared it a work of art and paid *two pounds ten* for it. I was amazed at the sum, but Jarge didn't even blink. He was a true collector.

By the time we'd cleared the straits, Jarge had tried that evil eye on everyone on board ship—includin' me. Scared the bejesus outta me, and I'd already seen the blasted thing. Jarge even snuck into the galley one night and scared the cook nearly to kingdom come. 'Course, all of us told him to lay off or we'd brain him. All of us 'cept a little Cockney feller name of Bell.

Everyone called Bell "Ding Dong" on account of his name. He didn't seem to mind the nickname, but he sure minded that evil eye. Nearly shriveled up with fright each time Jarge appeared with it. I thought he would go mad, the way he shook and babbled about the Devil and crossed himself like a Catholic

THE FATAL GLASS EYE

even though he weren't a religious man. Jarge was tickled to death by Ding Dong Bell's reaction and took to plaguing the life outta him, putting the "evil eye" on him whenever he passed until Ding Dong truly thought he was bewitched.

The other men were delighted with this entertainment and told Ding Dong Bell that he had to steal the evil eye. 'Course, Jarge knew what they said and was too crafty for Ding Dong. But the harder it was to steal, the more Ding Dong believed that stealing the eye was the only way to lift the curse. He was always trying to pick Jarge's pockets, and once he even tried to take the eye when Jarge was asleep. Jarge threw him under the bunk that time.

After that night Jarge started wearing the evil eye all the time—to protect it, he claimed. But I think Jarge was beginning to hate the Cockney, who treated him as if he were the Devil himself. Jarge grew mighty tired of seein' Ding Dong Bell cross himself every time he appeared, and it made him real mad when the other men got to believing Ding Dong might be right. It got so bad that the first mate wouldn't let Jarge and Ding Dong share a watch, seeing how they hated each other so.

Well, by the time we got into Port Said, Jarge had got to believing in that there evil eye himself. I saw him muttering over it more 'n once, and I know for a fact that he was trying to curse ol' Ding Dong to death with it before the voyage was over. While we was lyin' there in the roadstead one morning at Port Said, Jarge went aloft on a footrope to scrape a spar. Well, something musta fetched loose, 'cause suddenly I heard a yell, and when I turned around, Jarge was plummeting forty feet headfirst onto the deck. Cracked his skull open like an eggshell and his evil eye came rolling out.

This was Ding Dong Bell's chance, and he took it. He darted out from a corner and grabbed up the eye real fast. When he saw the mate running toward us, he popped the eye into his mouth to hide it from the mate. In less than a minute, ol' Ding Dong Bell started shivering and fell dead on the deck, right beside poor Jarge. The mate was mystified, but figured maybe Jarge had hit Ding Dong as he fell. 'Course I knew better, but I kept my mouth shut. Ding Dong Bell musta bit into that poisoned eye when he put it in his mouth.

What with Jarge and Ding Dong both being dead, I figured maybe there was something in that evil eye business after all, and I was real glad it was gone.

28

The Man Who Could Send Rats

NEW HAMPSHIRE

"I hate rats," I said furiously, sweeping away the small corpse our cat had laid on the doorstep.

"Our cats have always been good ratters," said Grandma from her rocking chair. "They are all descendants of Midnight, of course, which explains it."

"Explains what?" I asked, shutting the door and putting the broom away.

"Why, our cats are good ratters," said Grandma, knitting away furiously as she rocked. The sun lit up her graying hair as she smiled at me. "You're too young to remember, Amelia, when your granddad and I ran a boardinghouse. Those were busy days, those were. We had all sorts of folk a-comin' and a-goin' during those days, mostly loggers and railway men. They'd stay a few days, then move on, and someone else would take their place.

"Well, back in those days we could never keep a cat around the place. They all seemed to go plumb crazy in one way or another. Our first cat had fits. It would run in circles chasing its tail till it dropped onto the floor from exhaustion. Soon as it recovered, 'round it would go again. The cat finally ran away. Our next cat attacked the walls, banging against them until it knocked itself out. One day it hit the kitchen wall so hard its neck broke. Our third cat was a scratcher. He'd purr as sweet as you please and then claw you. We got rid of him because we didn't want him scratchin' your pa, who was jest a wee baby back then. We were finished with cats after that one—leastways, that's what we said."

"So when did you get Midnight?"

"We didn't get Midnight till after Jean-Claude came to the boardinghouse." Grandma paused and gave me a mysterious smile. She wanted me to ask her about Jean-Claude, I could tell.

"Who was Jean-Claude?" I asked on cue, pulling a chair up to the window and getting out my embroidery hoop.

"Jean-Claude was the Man Who Could Send Rats," Grandma said promptly. "Leastways, that's what he said."

"The Man Who Could Send Rats?" I exclaimed, intrigued. "What does that mean?"

"Jest what it implies. He claimed that he could make rats go anywhere he pleased, jest using the power of his mind. Not, to my thinkin', a very nice talent, and so I told him. But he jest laughed and said his talent came in real handy sometimes."

"But Gran, who exactly was Jean-Claude?" I repeated my original question.

"Jean-Claude was a logger. He came down from French Canada for the winter and put in at a loggin' camp hereabouts. When I met him, he had jest finished up his winter's work and wanted a place to board for a coupla days before headin' home. He'd been a long time in camp, and was real dirty and unkempt

177

when he arrived at the house. He wanted me to do his wash for him, but I was firm about that. We had plenty of folk who hired out to do the washing for loggers, and I wasn't going to do no one's washing for him. I had enough work what with runnin' the boardinghouse and takin' care of yer pa. Jean-Claude was none too pleased with this. He didn't want to spend no money, so he asked if he could do his own washing, and I let him.

"Then, a few days later, when it came time to settle the bill, that rascal didn't want to pay fifty cents a day for his room and board. Now, that was the rate we charged everybody, but he kept saying we were chargin' too much for a poor workingman and offered me twenty-five cents. Twenty-five cents! It were an insult to all our hard work! Well, I says to him, 'Everyone else pays up without complainin'. This is my regular price and it always has been. So you jest pay your bill like everyone else, and be grateful! I should be chargin' you more seein' as how you ate enough for two men.'

"So Jean-Claude paid up fair and square. But he was mad clean through. Such a black look he gave me as he left.

"Well, I forgot all about Jean-Claude after that 'cause a load of railway men came that afternoon, and the boardinghouse was filled to the rafters. It wasn't till late that night, when everyone was asleep, that the rats came. The whole house was filled with pounding and scraping noises. It sounded like someone was moving a heavy trunk across the floor and throwing furniture around. But it was rats, hundreds of rats moving into the walls of the boardinghouse. The sound was so loud, everyone had a hard time sleepin' that night, and the next morning all the boarders wanted to know if we had heard the terrible banging and scratching. The railway men thought we had a ghost.

THE MAN WHO COULD SEND RATS

"'Course, we investigated right away, and found all them rats everywhere. I remembered Jean-Claude then, let me tell you. He went away mad, and he musta sent every rat from all the towns 'round here to our place. And us with no cats, 'count of them all taking fits when they lived here.

"Well, those railway men were jest plumb nice. They set down and tried to figure out how to help us. One man said he heard if you stole a cat, that cat wouldn't catch no sickness that the other cats had before. The other fellows thought we were feeding our cats too much meat. So the railway men put their heads together, and by that evenin', Midnight appeared in our kitchen. She was a pretty black cat with white paws and a white patch on her chest. The railway men claimed she was a stray that they found wandering around town 'bout two miles away. We decided not to question them too closely, seein' as the one man who suggested stealin' a cat seemed a bit uncomfortable talkin' about it.

"Well, that Midnight started catchin' rats right away. I reckoned she musta thought our boardinghouse was a huntin' paradise, what with rats everywhere and all the railway men 'round to make a fuss when she caught one. The only strange thing 'bout Midnight was that she would never eat the rats she caught. Though, lookin' back on it, I think that wasn't too bad after all, seein' as how the railway men thought too much meat was behind the fits our other cats took. But it left a powerful lot of little corpses about the place.

"That Midnight could catch up to fifteen rats a night. But she would get tired toward the end of the evening. Once she was tired, she wouldn't kill no more rats. She'd jest drag them into the kitchen and leave them for us to chase with a broom when we got up to light the morning fire. The boarders liked all the commotion we made, chasing rats with the broom. They used to get up early jest to watch us, and they laughed and laughed. They took to purchasing extra cream for Midnight and sneaking it to her, thinking we didn't know!

"Well, it took three months to clear out all them rats. And when Midnight had her first litter of kittens, every one of them was claimed before they was even born.

"The next fall, when Jean-Claude came to our door wanting to board, I sent him packin' real quick. He'd been walkin' in the rain and was soaked to the skin, but I didn't feel one bit sorry for him. 'You're the one what sent them rats here last spring,' I says. 'You best clear out of here now before my husband breaks your neck.'

"He didn't say a word, jest walked away real quick down the road, and never came back our way again."

"And that's why Midnight's descendants are such good ratters," I finished.

Grandma grinned at me. "Yes, indeed," said she.

29

Old Betty Booker

KITTERY, MAINE

Skipper Perkins was so tight with his money that you needed a chisel to pry it out of his fist. So when Old Betty Booker came to the dock early one morning and said, "Bring me a bit o' halibut, Skipper Perkins," his reply was short and to the point: "Show me your sixpence, ma'am, and I'll show you some fish."

This wasn't the most tactful answer to make to the local witch. Most of the other skippers made sure to slip Old Betty Booker a few haddock on the house whenever she came asking. But Skipper Perkins was so thrifty he would have charged the Good Lord himself if He'd come a-knockin' for some fish. So he certainly took no mind of Old Betty Booker, standing on the dock with an ill-bodin' scowl on her rugged face as she watched his ship sail away into the dawn while the wind blew her raggedy gray hair this way and that. Finally Old Betty Booker made a grasping motion with her hand, as if to capture the wind. Then she blew it away across her palm in the direction Skipper Perkins had taken his ship.

And from that moment, Skipper Perkins was plagued with bad luck. His men fell ill. A gale tore up his sails while the waves battered his ship up and down, and the fish wouldn't bite. He came home poorer than he left.

Soon after he got home, a rumor reached Skipper Perkins that shook him down to his skinflint core. Old Betty Booker was making a witch-bridle out of horsehair, strands of tow, and the bark of yellow birch, and every bit of her bridle had Skipper Perkins's name on it. She was planning on riding Skipper Perkins like a horse, away down to York Harbor on a night of her choosing.

Well, Skipper Perkins got into quite a panic when he heard the news. He took to double-barrin' his door at night and making sure he was home before sunset. Not that these precautions kept him from shiverin' and shakin' all night long in fear of Old Betty Booker and her witch-bridle. Then one morning a message came from Old Betty Booker. She was brewin' up a storm in her warming pan. When the storm was done, she would set it free, and during that storm she was going to ride Skipper Perkins down to York Harbor with her witch bridle.

The storm came right on schedule, a-howlin' and a-blowin' as fierce as ever it could be. The creek was a-floodin' and the wind nearly bendin' the trees in half. Inside their houses, people were huddled around damp fireplaces and prayin' that Old Betty Booker would not remember them that night.

As for Skipper Perkins, well, he was double-bolted inside his house and every movable piece of furniture he possessed was piled up against the door. Then he hid himself under the bed and waited for Old Betty Booker. The wind was shriekin' down the chimney and rattlin' against the windows, and the rain was beatin' on the roof so hard a body could hardly think

OLD BETTY BOOKER

for the noise of it. But through the almighty racket of the storm, Skipper Perkins could hear a devilish wailing that could only be Old Betty Booker.

"Bring me a bit o' halibut, Skipper Perkins."

The front door began rattlin', and he heard the sound of witch-claws scratchin' on the walls. Slipping out from under the bed, Skipper Perkins rushed to push the furniture tighter against the rattlin' door.

"Bring me a bit o' halibut, Skipper Perkins," Old Betty Booker howled. The gale seemed to rise up and howl with her. The door shook fiercely and began to open. Rain came pelting in, and Skipper Perkins could hear the chattering of the witches just outside. He kept pushing against the furniture in sheer panic, his bare feet sliding slowly back and back as the door opened.

Suddenly Skipper Perkins gave a yelp of terror and leapt for the bed. He dived under the covers, shakin' in fear. With the resistance gone, the door popped open and the witches came troopin' inside, led by Old Betty Booker, holding the witch-bridle and a whip.

"Bring me a bit o' halibut, Skipper Perkins," she cackled, pulling him, covers and all, off the bed. Skipper Perkins stared up into her wild eyes, quaking in terror.

The witches stripped off his nightclothes and held him down as Old Betty Booker bridled him up. Then Old Betty Booker climbed up on his back, and the other witches climbed up on top of hers, and with a crack of the whip Skipper Perkins was trotting through the gale in a blind panic, heading for York Harbor.

The night was as wild as they come, but not nearly as wild as the witches riding atop Skipper Perkins. They cackled and shouted and cursed, and when he slowed their witch-claws bit into him, making him shriek and run faster. When he staggered into York Harbor, Old Betty Booker made Skipper Perkins turn 'round and take them back to Kittery.

It wasn't until the darkest hour, just before cockcrow, that Old Betty Booker released Skipper Perkins from the witch-bridle. He collapsed next to his front door, more dead than alive, and lay looking up into her wild face, too tired to be frightened. She said: "Don't you go chargin' sixpence to a poor old woman no more, Skipper Perkins." Then Old Betty Booker and her witch-familiars vanished into the dark, and the storm went with them. Skipper Perkins crawled through his front door, past the mound of furniture, and curled up in the blankets, too worn to climb onto his bed.

For three weeks Skipper Perkins lay abed, nursin' his wounds and telling his story to the wonderin' neighbors. When he finally got up, the first thing he did was catch a mess of halibut and send them over to Old Betty Booker, free of charge.

30

Black Magic

He was a strange man, wild-eyed and hook-nosed, with a shock of black curls streaked with gray and the loping walk and crazy laugh of the insane. Folks in town avoided Mad Henry, who engaged in no visible profession yet somehow always had money. He lived in a large, decrepit mansion, from which strange lights shone at night. Folks said he was a black magician who called upon the powers of darkness to wreak havoc upon his neighbors. Others claimed he was a mad doctor trying to restore life to foul corpses he dug up from the local cemetery. Rumors spread across the whole region regarding Mad Henry, but no one ever dared ask him what it was he did in his lonely mansion at night.

Young boys looking for a thrill looked no further than the windows of that benighted dwelling. Strange and grotesque shapes could be seen through the curtains when the moon was full, and many a tough lad went running from the place, weeping with fright. Most of them spent the next month plagued by the nightmarish memories of what they had seen.

Now it happened one year that a new attorney opened an office in town, bringing with him his young family. The eldest daughter, Rachel, was a beauty and soon became the belle of local society. Mad Henry saw her through his bedroom window one night as she strolled arm-in-arm with two of her girlfriends, and he fell in love with the red-haired minx at once with all the passion in his twisted soul. The very next evening, he showed up on her doorstep carrying a bunch of red roses that gleamed with their own inner light and left dewdrops of pure gold on the maiden's mantelpiece long after their giver made his way home.

Rachel was both intrigued and frightened by her strange suitor, who was so very much older than she. Her father was pleased by her new beau. Yes, Mad Henry was a strange fellow, but he was obviously well-off and could keep his daughter in the style she deserved. And he showered the lovely red-haired maiden with gifts—goblets of pure gold, necklaces of pearl and diamond, and stranger things, too. Like the statue of a small dog that could actually bark and wag its tail; a mirror that reflected far-off vistas when it was not being used by its owner; and a pot of daisies—Rachel's favorite flower—that never grew old nor dropped a single petal, even if it was not watered for a week.

The gifts made Rachel uneasy. She couldn't help wondering what price their owner had paid to create them. Folks in town whispered that Mad Henry had sold his soul to the Devil in exchange for the ability to turn lead into gold. Alchemist, they called him, and other, darker names. He never invited Rachel or her parents into his home. He never brought anyone there, and Rachel was afraid to ask why.

About this time, young Geoffrey Simmons, the son of a prominent businessman in town, came home from university, where he was studying to be a doctor. He met Rachel at a party

BLACK MAGIC

given in his honor and fell head-over-heels for the attorney's daughter. Rachel found his simple love much easier to accept than the complex adoration offered to her by the alchemist. A week after they met, Geoffrey and Rachel eloped, leaving behind a bewildered and angry father and a stunned alchemist.

The elopement was a nine-day wonder in town. By the time Geoffrey and Rachel returned from their honeymoon, their marriage was an accepted fact, and though they were teased about its suddenness, everyone was happy for them. Rachel's parents threw a big ball for the newlyweds and invited everyone in town. It was a festive, happy occasion with music and dancing and special performers brought to town for the festivities.

Rachel had been acting jittery all evening, looking over her shoulder again and again, sitting out the dances, and laughing with a too-high pitch that suggested the red-haired bride was not really happy at all. Geoffrey noticed and pulled her into a small alcove to kiss and comfort her.

"Are you worried about Henry?" Geoffrey asked.

Rachel turned her head and nodded in agreement.

"Henry won't come," Geoffrey said. "He's a gentleman and will leave you alone."

"You don't know him," Rachel told her new husband. "He is not quite sane, Geoffrey. He will come for me."

"Nonsense!" Geoffrey scoffed gently. He gave her another kiss and then the couple returned to the dance.

Rachel was waltzing with her father when she heard the first clap of thunder. It boomed in the distance and gradually got louder, until it became a continuous roar in the sky above the dance hall. Lightning flashed again and again, sizzling the air, but no rain fell. It was not that kind of storm.

The guests murmured in fear as the sound of the storm grew louder than the orchestra, and the music twanged and limped to a halt when lightning struck a tree directly outside the hall. Suddenly, the double doors blew open and a sharp, nasty breeze whirled in, bringing with it the smell of dead, decaying things and just a whiff of acrid chemicals. And then Mad Henry loomed in the doorway, black cape flapping in the foul breeze, pupils gleaming red with anger, wild black curls streaked with gray standing on end. He raised his arms above his head and shouted aloud in a language that made the eyes burn and the skin shiver.

There came a sharp clanking sound, and the grotesque figures of the dead came marching two by two into the room, decaying skeletons with bits of skin and dirt still clinging to them. Their eye sockets glowed with blue fire as they surrounded the crowd. Guests screamed in terror and raced to escape out of every door and window. The boldest tried to attack the invaders, but those who tried found themselves pinned against the walls by hands of stretched gray skin and white bone.

Two of the creatures captured Geoffrey and threw him down at the feet of their lord amidst a shower of dirt and bits of gray skin that flaked from their foul forms. Geoffrey's head banged against the stone floor with a crack that left him stunned and helpless before the alchemist. Mad Henry stared at his rival with a gentle smile that boded ill for the university student. "Kill him," he ordered. "And bring me his widow."

Rachel screamed then, a terrible sound that made even the wild skeletons flinch. She ran forward, pushing through the confining ring of the dead, and flung herself upon her trembling young husband.

"Kill us both," she cried desperately, holding her husband close. "I will not go with you."

Mad Henry smiled grimly and nodded to his dead servants. They plucked the red-haired lass from her husband as if she weighed no more than a small child and marched her out the door. Her father leapt at the cadavers, beating at them with his walking stick, and one struck out with a decaying fist, striking the attorney a blow that broke his nose and sent shards of bone directly into his brain, killing him instantly. They carried the screaming, beating, writhing Rachel out into the thundering night, and none could stay their progress or pull the girl from their grisly hands.

Red eyes gleaming with evil satisfaction, Mad Henry drew a silver-bladed knife and casually cut the bridegroom's throat from ear to ear. The he whirled around, cape swirling about him like a black cloud, and strode from the room. Behind him, the army of the dead tossed their battered victims to the floor and followed their master, striding right through the large pool of blood that poured from the dying Geoffrey as he gasped out the final breaths of his life. Behind them, the monsters left a trail of blood-stained footprints, half human and half skeleton, that burned themselves permanently into the stone floor of the dance hall.

Geoffrey's parents rushed to his side, and his mother pressed a handkerchief to the gaping wound on his throat in an ineffectual attempt to stop the bleeding. He gazed up at them with glazing eyes and gasped: "Find Rachel." And then he was gone.

The sounds of thunder and lightning were fading away as the alchemist and his dead companions disappeared into the dark night. Geoffrey's father patted his wife clumsily on the shoulder, went home for his gun, and then stalked through the streets of the town, heading toward the house of the local minister, who had stayed home from the party that night with a headache. Geoffrey's father didn't care if the man were dropping dead from consumption. He was determined to rouse the holy man at once and rescue his daughter-in-law.

As Geoffrey's father marched across town, he was joined by Rachel's two brothers, a cousin, and the fathers of her friends. The small mob pounded on the door of the minister's house, waking him and his wife and demanding he come with them at once to the home of the alchemist. They did not even give the poor preacher time to dress, dragging him along with them in nightshirt and cap, his glasses on upside-down and a Bible clutched in his hands.

When they arrived at the alchemist's house, they found it lit from top to bottom, and the stench of chemicals set all the men to gasping for breath and sneezing. Geoffrey's father seemed oblivious to the smell. He leapt into the house with his rifle, shouting aloud for Mad Henry to come down. Inspired by his courage, the mob spread out through the well-lit house, searching for the alchemist and his prisoner. They found nothing. Nothing at all. No furniture, no laboratory, not even dust and cobwebs. The house was completely empty save for the light, which shone from a series of mysterious globes that bobbed near the ceiling of each room. The alchemist had vanished.

The maddened mob torched the empty house and dragged the minister for miles through the surrounding woods and farms and fields, searching for Mad Henry and his prisoner. But they were gone. Search parties scoured the countryside for days, but turned up nothing. Geoffrey and Rachel's father were buried in the local cemetery, and the dance hall, whose stone floor was scored with the footprints of the dead, was torn down. No one in town spoke about what had happened, and no one dared imagine what had become of poor Rachel.

A year to the day after the ball, a timid knock sounded upon the door of Geoffrey's parents' home. When the father opened it, he saw a gaunt, gray figure on the stoop. Her eyes were dull with exhaustion and pain; her once-red hair was pure white and writhed wildly about her head. It took him a moment to realize that it was Rachel, but his wife knew at once and pulled the wretched figure into the house with exclamations of horror and pity. Rachel couldn't speak. Her tongue had been cut out. But she produced a knife from her tattered garments—the knife with a silver blade that they had last seen in the hands of the alchemist—and the gleam of satisfaction in Rachel's eyes told them that the streaks of blood that coated the knife were those of Mad Henry. Then Rachel fell into a dead faint. Geoffrey's parents carried her to their son's old room and summoned a doctor and her mother. But it was too late. Rachel died in her sleep that night, and upon her ravaged face was a smile of peace.

Inside her tattered dress, they found a note to her mother. It read:

Dearest Mother:
After many months of imprisonment and terrible suffering at the hands of the alchemist, I dug myself out of the stone tower where he kept me, clawing my

way through loose mortar and stone until I was free. After his last gruesome visit to my cell, I followed the alchemist to his home deep in the dark woods near the tower. Mad Henry had taken my husband and my youth, and I was determined to take his life. And so I have, using the knife he used to kill my Geoffrey. If this condemns me in the eyes of God, so be it. I will die a murderess, and proud to be. Geoffrey and my father have been avenged, and I leave it to God to judge if I have done right or wrong.

Yours,
Rachel

31

The Devil and Jonathan Moulton

HAMPTON, NEW HAMPSHIRE

General Jonathan Moulton was known throughout New England as a great warrior and a fine man. But every man has his Achilles' heel, and the general was a tad too fond of money for his own good.

One day the general was sitting next to the fireplace in the sitting room thinking about his life, and he up and remarked that he wouldn't mind selling his soul to the Devil if only he could be filthy rich. Now, the Devil was not about to pass up such an opportunity as this. Before the general could say another word, the Devil had whisked down the chimney in a shower of sparks and was at the man's elbow, dressed in black velvet from tip to toe and showing not a smudge despite his dramatic entrance.

"Well I'll be hanged," quoth the general, somewhat in shock.

"Not today," said the Devil suavely. "Perhaps in the future. But we must hurry to business, General, for I am due at the governor's home in but fifteen minutes." The Devil picked up a hot coal and elegantly consulted his watch. "Time, I see, is passing quickly." He tossed the coal back into the fire.

The general was a bit taken aback by this revelation. Portsmouth was a good five leagues from Hampton, and a person who had the arrogance to assume he could make it from here to there in under fifteen minutes was either insane or . . .

"Devil take me for a fool!" shouted the general.

"I plan to," he replied, so softly that the general, in his excitement, did not hear him.

"You, sir, cannot really be the—"

"Now, General, what's in a name?" The Devil waved his hand expressively. "Come. I believe you proposed a bargain?"

At the word *bargain*, the general went on the alert. His favorite boast was that neither man nor Devil could best him in a trade. And now he had the chance to prove it. He settled back in his chair and assumed a casual air. He even pulled out his jackknife and began whittling on a small stick from the wood box by the hearth. Not to be outdone, the Devil pulled out a jackknife, a twin to the general's, and started paring his fingernails. The general looked up after a moment and pretended to be surprised that the Devil was still there.

"Well, sir," he began, "I do seem to recall mentioning a bargain. But I have no proof that you can keep such a bargain, now, do I?" He frowned fiercely, his bushy eyebrows meeting over his nose, the very portrait of a man who will not be taken in by appearances.

The Devil casually ran a hand through his pockets and produced a fist full of gold. He tossed the gold in the air, and the coins scattered to the four corners of the room. The general's eyes almost popped out of his head. He scrambled quickly to grab one, but no sooner had his fingers closed over it than he dropped it with a yell. It was scorching hot! He turned reproachfully to the Devil.

The Devil chuckled. "Try it again," he said.

"I'm no fool," said the general tartly.

This remark brought a hearty laugh from the Devil. "Go ahead," he cried merrily.

The general cautiously touched the tip of one finger to a gold coin. It was cool. The general picked it up and bit it. Tasted like gold. He weighed it in his hand. Yes, it was the right weight. He rang it on the table, and the sound was true. A huge smile crept across his face. It was gold. He flung himself to the floor and gathered up every coin in feverish haste.

The Devil watched him with a wicked smile. "Satisfied, General?" he asked.

General Moulton sat upon the floor with his fists full of gold. "Completely," he said, stuffing the gold into his pockets and searching about for any coins he might have missed.

"Well, then. Before we conclude our bargain, do you have something to drink in this place? I am parched," the Devil complained.

"There's some rum in the cupboard," the general said, picking up a last coin that had rolled under his chair.

"Excellent," said the Devil, seating himself elegantly in a chair and adjusting his cloak so that the general could clearly see the jeweled clasp. The general brought the decanter and two glasses from the cupboard and poured his guest a drink. He had it in mind to get the Devil drunk and so cheat him out of the gold in his pocket, but the Devil, sipping the rum like a connoisseur, gave him a knowing look, and he quickly put it out of his mind. "Does Your Excellency not like it?" the general asked quickly.

THE DEVIL AND JONATHAN MOULTON

"It needs a little kick," said the Devil. He touched a taper to the rum and it burst into flame. The general saw with horror that the flames resembled an adder. The flame-adder flicked its forked tongue at the general as the Devil proposed a toast: "To our better acquaintance." The Devil quaffed the drink in a single gulp.

The general shuddered, but he took a small sip so as not to offend his guest.

The Devil put down the glass and said in a suddenly businesslike manner: "Now, I think you have seen for yourself that I can make you the richest man in the province. So, in return for your agreement, duly signed and sealed, to deliver your soul to me"—he drew a thick parchment from his pocket—"I will engage, on my part, to fill your boots with gold such as you have received here tonight, on the first day of each month."

The Devil laid the scroll on the table between them, smoothing it straight with hands that glittered with diamonds. The sight of those jewels made the general's eyes gleam.

"But mark me well, General," the Devil said, narrowing his eyes. "If you try to trick me, you will repent of it. I know you of old, Jonathan Moulton."

The general flinched and drew back at this declaration. Then a new thought seemed to strike him, for he straightened his shoulders and brightened a little.

The Devil dipped a pen into the inkhorn and held it out. "Sign," said he.

The general hesitated. The Devil smiled slightly. The general's pockets suddenly emptied. "What the devi . . . blazes?!" he cried.

The gold reappeared on the table right beside the parchment.

"Sign," said the Devil again.

The general seized the pen. His hand was shaking violently. He took a gulp of rum, which steadied him. Then, with an encouraging nod from the Devil and a quick glance at the pile of gold, General Moulton signed his name. Scanning the fatal parchment, he was astonished to see many of the prominent men of his day listed upon it.

"At least I shall be in good company," he muttered to himself.

"Very good," the Devil said, rising from his chair and placing the scroll carefully in his pocket. "You may rely on me, General. Do not forget to leave your boots on the crane in the fireplace the evening before the first day of the month." So saying, the Devil flung his cloak about him and disappeared up the chimney.

The very next day the general put his little scheme into action. If he were going to sell his soul for boots full of gold, then he was going to find the biggest boots that were ever made and make the Devil fill them each month. He ransacked the town, looking for the largest pair of boots he could find.

The townsfolk thought it a bit odd when the general started paying them to look at their shoes, but money is money, and the general was very persuasive. He finally located a pair of trooper's jackboots that came up to the wearer's thigh. Paying the man handsomely, Moulton hung these boots on the crane in the fireplace the evening before the first day of the month. Not without a twinge, mind you, for he remembered the Devil's warning. But if the Devil rebuked him, the general was prepared to remind him that the contract simply specified boots, not boot size nor previous owner thereof.

When the general went to the fireplace the next morning, he found the huge boots filled to the top with gold. He was elated. He had managed to trick the Devil after all!

From that moment on General Jonathan Moulton was rolling in wealth. It was uncanny how quickly he became rich, and how everything he touched seemed to prosper. His neighbors, regarding him with an envy that slowly changed to aversion and fear, decided that no one could be so lucky by chance. Folks began whispering that the general must have made a pact with the Devil to gain such wealth. Others replied: "What does it matter? The general could outwit the Devil himself."

This speech, when repeated to the general, caused him to laugh heartily.

He liked to take out the huge boots now and then and give them a quick polish, chuckling to himself over his clever trick. A new plan was taking shape in his mind. He would outwit the Devil again, and in the process become so rich he could buy his way into heaven. The general laughed to himself as he hung up the boots that night.

Early the next morning the Devil came to the top of the chimney as usual to fill the general's boots per their agreement. He poured gold down the chimney into the boots, but it was like pouring water down a drain. No matter how much gold the Devil poured in, the level in the boots never increased. Those blasted boots could not be filled. The Devil scratched his head reflectively. Something was amiss. He hopped into the chimney and was immediately stopped by a giant pile of gold. So the Devil whisked himself into the chamber through a window and found himself knee-deep in gold.

Furious, the Devil waded to the chimney through the gleaming pile of gold and tore the boots from the crane. He saw at once that their soles had been cut off, leaving only the legs for him to fill. The Devil stood for a long time, staring at what was left of the huge boots. *Give a man an inch*, he reflected. A nasty smile lit up his face, and he disappeared.

That night the general's house burned to the ground. The general barely managed to escape with the clothes on his back. He cursed and raged at the Devil, for all his gold had been secreted throughout the house and was now going up in flames. But the man calmed down after a moment, realizing that the gold would melt and he would find a solid lump of it in the cellar come daybreak.

By dawn he was working feverishly to move the ash and rubble from the ruined cellar. He dared not accept help from his neighbors, for how would he explain so much gold? But when the rubble was cleared, there was no sign of the gold. It had vanished without a trace.

So poor General Moulton, once the bravest soldier in the province, was left without his home, without his gold, and with a forfeit soul. Which just goes to show, you can't trick the Devil.

After the general died, there were so many rumors about his contract with the Devil that the authorities finally opened his grave to quiet them. But when the lid was removed, the coffin was empty.

32

The Frogs of Windham

WINDHAM, CONNECTICUT

Lawyer Elderkin stood on the porch looking up at the night sky. Clouds were rolling in, obscuring the stars, but for a few moments the moon still shone on the sleepy town of Windham. Elderkin fervently hoped that the clouds meant rain. There was a severe drought in the county, and if it didn't rain soon, the farmers would be in trouble. He drew in a deep breath, enjoying the smell of the honeysuckle growing on the trellis.

"Mister Elderkin," called his wife from the doorway, "it is time for good folk to be in bed. It's always late you are," she added teasingly, her Irish lilt becoming stronger as she came out onto the porch and tucked her hand into his arm. "If you're not careful, you'll be late for the last trump! Now come to bed."

Lawyer Elderkin smiled down at his still-beautiful wife. In the last gleams of moonlight, she looked as young as a girl, not like a woman expecting her first grandchild. The clouds encompassed the moon, and the light faded from the porch.

"By all means, Mistress Elderkin. Let us go to bed." He raised his eyebrows at her and she giggled.

The Elderkins retired to their room and to their well-deserved slumbers. Outside, a light wind stirred the trees and knocked lightly against the windows of the town. The town quieted down as the weary townsfolk snuggled into their beds and sank into peaceful repose, while the east wind danced through the dark clouds and whistled in the meadow outside town.

It was just after midnight when the silence was broken by a terrible noise coming from the sky overhead. The screaming, screeching, roaring sound was like none ever heard by the townsfolk. They came tumbling out of their beds in fright.

"Injuns!" shouted Mister Smith, the owner of the local shop, to his cowering wife. "It's got to be Injuns. Get the children and go down to the cellar." He grabbed his gun and ran down to the street, still in his nightclothes. He joined a growing crowd of people, most of them still in their nightclothes, a few wearing nothing but the covers from their beds. Some of the men were searching each building in town, trying to find the cause of the terrible noise that still roared overhead. A few carried guns, and these men banded together with Mister Smith to search for Indians.

"It's the Last Judgment!" a woman screamed, and her words were echoed throughout the crowd. Children were crying and shouting, women were wringing their hands, and the minister was praying loudly over a devoted knot of folk who were on their knees.

The Elderkins joined the terrified crowd, holding hands tightly so as not to be separated. Above them the terrible screeching and roaring intensified. And in it, they could hear a name. *Colonel Dyer. Colonel Dyer.* Lawyer Elderkin gasped. That was the name of his rival, the only other lawyer in town. And then he heard it. His own name came through the roaring, screeching sky. *Elderkin. Elderkin. Colonel Dyer. Colonel Dyer.*

The people nearest the Elderkins backed away. "The Devil has come for them," a little boy screamed and ran for his mother.

"Nonsense," shouted Colonel Dyer, shoving his way through the crowd to the Elderkins and pulling his frightened wife behind him. Mistresses Dyer and Elderkin, who usually treated each other with a marked coolness of manner, clung to one another like sisters.

"We are God-fearing people. Even if the Devil wanted to claim us, the Lord would save us!" shouted Lawyer Elderkin.

Above the town, the roaring continued. *Colonel Dyer. Elderkin. Elderkin. Colonel Dyer.* And then a terrible screeching made everyone cover their ears.

"It's Injuns, not the Devil," shouted Mister Smith, thrusting his way through the crowd, waving his gun. "Come on, men. Let's get 'em before they attack!"

He led his band of Indian hunters toward the hills outside the town limits. Many of the townsfolk, hearing his words, ran back into their homes and barred their doors. But the Elderkins and the Dyers hurried over to the minister, more frightened than they would admit by the continuing repetition of their names from the roaring sky. The minister prayed over them, asking God to keep them safe from whatever devilry was seeking them by name.

Atop the hill outside of town, the Indian hunters quickly realized that the sounds were coming from the east rather than the sky. Seeing no Indians, the men beat a hasty retreat from the terrible roaring, not wanting to be involved in whatever devilry was taking place.

Gradually, the sound lessened. The repetition of the names *Colonel Dyer* and *Elderkin* faded away into a continuous, dull

THE FROGS OF WINDHAM

roaring. After hearing Mister Smith's report on the source of the sound, the minister walked to the eastern boundary of town and prayed for the protection of the people. This prayer, coupled with the gradual lessening of the sound, reduced the panic, and most people went back to their own homes.

The Elderkins sat on their front porch with the Dyers, waiting for the terrible sounds to fade away completely. Toward dawn all was again silent but for the wind blowing in the trees.

At dawn Colonel Dyer and Lawyer Elderkin, along with Mister Smith, the minister, and a few other bold folk, set off eastward in search of the source of the terrible disturbance. About three-quarters of a mile outside town, they came to the millpond. They stopped and looked down upon the source of the terrible roaring sound. The pond was nearly dry except for a deep ditch that ran through it. And surrounding the ditch were the bodies of thousands of bullfrogs, which had waged a terrible and prolonged battle during the night for possession of the remaining water in the pond. Even now a few stubborn frogs on the north side of the ditch were crawling toward their enemies, croaking a battle cry that sounded remarkably like *Colonel Dyer*, while the ones to the south responded with a cry of *Elderkin too, Elderkin too*. The atmospheric conditions of the night before had magnified the sound so that it seemed to be coming from the sky above the town.

After a moment's stunned silence, the men laughed until the tears rolled down their cheeks and Colonel Dyer had to be picked up off the road. Dyer and Elderkin each claimed one of the remaining belligerent frogs to offer as proof of the source of the sound. And ever after, the lawyers delighted in producing their strange pets and telling the story of the fighting frogs of Windham.

33

Tom Dunn's Dance

WOBURN, MASSACHUSETTS

Tom Dunn was a rascal of a fellow who would rather drink and dance than go to church, but he was a favorite with the ladies, being tall and handsome. Tom went to all the social events, and was very popular. Still, the minister and the deacons all shook their heads over his behavior, fearing for his immortal soul if he kept up his rascally ways.

One fine night Tom attended the local husking bee. He was in high spirits that night, for there was plenty to drink, and he had a pretty partner. The only low point came when the minister took him aside for a few moments to talk about his immortal soul and the mending of his ways. But a few drinks cured Tom of his uneasiness, and after he had shucked twenty red ears of corn and claimed twenty kisses from his pretty partner as payment for them, Tom was on top of the world. Feeling self-satisfied and rather reckless, he decided to take a shortcut home, even though it meant going over Rag Rock at night.

Now, everyone knew that Rag Rock was the home of terrible spirits and many demon-kind. Legend said that underneath Rag Rock, an evil spirit was holding the Indian maiden Nansema and her lover Winitihooloo captive inside a

209

glittering cave filled with treasure. Tom Dunn usually avoided Rag Rock, wanting nothing to do with demons, or with angels for that matter, not being fond of anything spiritual in nature. But on this night Tom just laughed at the old tales and went straight up the hill.

As Tom neared the top of Rag Rock, he heard the sound of a fiddle floating on the breeze. A light appeared among the trees, and he could hear laughter and the sound of feet shuffling in a dance.

Oh ho, he said to himself. *It seems that some of the so-called righteous townsfolk have got themselves up a moonlight dance. The minister should see this. After hearing the sacrilegious music they're playing, he won't be so quick to tell me I'm shaming the town.*

Tom pushed his way through the thicket, eager to see whom he had caught making merry on Rag Rock. A moment later he found himself on the edge of a clearing. Torches flared on every side, and there was a joyous crowd milling about and dancing in a spirited manner quite unlike any he had ever seen.

Now, Tom dearly enjoyed a good dance, and this one was better than the best of its kind. His toes tapped to the cheery fiddle tune as he gazed about in wonder. Then he gave a delighted laugh and strode boldly into the ring of dancers. He offered them an elaborate bow, and they greeted him with a friendly shout.

A girl with laughing black eyes and rosy red lips was sitting just outside the circle. She eyed him mischievously and twitched her skirt, allowing him to catch a glimpse of her pretty ankles. The invitation in her eyes and her flirtatious sidelong glance were all the incentive Tom needed to sweep her out of her seat and into the dance. Tom whirled her about in the wildest dance he had ever led. He seemed to be floating in the air, so light were his heels and so dashing his moves.

Soon an admiring ring had formed around Tom and his partner, inciting him to new heights and marvelous feats of skill. The fiddle seemed to put lightning in his heels; he could make no wrong move this night. He swung his partner around and they separated in order to dance back to each other across the field. Tom gave a mighty leap and a whirl, cracking his heels together. As he came to the ground, he noticed that his partner, who was dancing suggestively toward him, had changed. She looked older; her face had grown longer and her eyes were dark and hard. Tom twirled again, and now when he came face to face with his partner, he saw with dismay that she had transformed completely. Her form was lank and twisted, her hair wild and disarrayed, her teeth yellow and pointed, and her green eyes full of wickedness and glee.

In that moment Tom realized that he was in the company of the demon inhabitants of Rag Rock. His partner gave him a twisted smile as they joined hands, and the faces in the crowd were no longer noble, though they were still merry. Tom was trembling with such fear that his legs would barely hold him. But he knew if he stopped dancing now, his fate was sealed. The only way out for him was to dance until sunrise, or for a minister to order him to stop. But his minister was safe in bed, and Tom knew he had to dance or die.

Well, the fat was in the fire. Tom threw off his coat and tie and settled into a steady jig, fancy antics forgotten. The moon

TOM DUNN'S DANCE

was setting over the trees. If he could hold out for two more hours, he would be free. His partner giggled happily and tried to snuggle up to him, but he danced away from her. He could not escape the others so easily. Each way he turned, another gleaming pair of evil eyes, or a face not quite human, was watching him. Many of the demon-folk raised their glasses to him in a threatening toast.

By this time Tom was in agony. His muscles burned and his body was shaking with fatigue.

I must keep dancing, he told himself, urging himself on. No one else was dancing now. They were all watching him hungrily. The clearing was silent except for the obscenely merry sound of the fiddle.

Suddenly a cramp caught Tom in the calf. He doubled over in agony, and his onetime partner shouted with glee. She loomed above him, and a whiff of sulfur choked him. "God save me," shouted Tom, tumbling onto his back.

At the name of God, there came a sudden hissing sound. Tom heard growls and curses and had a brief vision of inhuman figures scurrying away. The witch, who was hanging greedily over him, burst into flames. The stink of sulfur and the blazing flames overwhelmed him, and Tom knew no more.

He woke at daybreak. He was lying in the dirt of an overgrown clearing, his coat and his tie next to him. His head pounded fiercely.

"Lord, what a hangover," he moaned, pushing himself up. "And what a terrible dream."

His jackknife fell out of his pocket as he spoke. He bent painfully to pick it up, then immediately dropped it with a terrified gasp. The face of the pretty girl with whom he had danced was etched on the handle. Kneeling down in the dirt, he picked up the knife again. Yes, it was she. Slowly he turned the knife over. On the other side was the picture of the witch as she'd looked right before he blacked out.

Feeling sick and feverish, Tom thrust the knife into his pocket, grabbed his things, and stumbled his way home. He lay in bed for a month with fever. When his health returned, Tom immediately joined the church, married his pretty partner from the husking bee, forsook all worldly entertainments, and never drank anything stronger than tea. The minister was delighted that Tom had taken his speech to heart, and ever afterward claimed credit for Tom's reformation.

Within a few years Tom was a deacon and was considered by all to be the most honest and upright workman in the community. If at times he vexed his wife with his refusal to attend any of the village dances, he was in all other respects a model husband. When he died, his wife put up a grand tombstone in his honor.

34

The Loup-Garou

When my grandpère came to Woonsocket from Canada, he thought he had finally left the loup-garou behind.

"Pierre, the loup-garou are men just like anybody else," Grandpère once told me. "But they've got into some kind of sinful behavior that makes them susceptible to the workings of the Devil. Once he's got them in his coils, the Devil transforms them into wolves and makes them do his work."

According to my grandpère, the loup-garou will catch a man and eat him when they can. It's always a good idea to check the shadows if you hear a loup-garou is about. The only way you can transform the loup-garou back into a man is to prick him with a knife till he bleeds. But no one had heard of loup-garou in Rhode Island, so Grandpère thought he was safe at last.

Well, one night my great-grandpère had a terrible spell and lay there moanin' and groanin' like he was dying. My grandpère knew he needed to get the priest mighty quick, so he hitched up his sleigh and set off through the long, dark woods. The night was silent except for the snow crunch, crunch, crunching under the horse's hooves and the swish of the runners. My grandpère, he was feeling badly for his father and was hurryin', hurryin', hurryin' as fast as he could go to get the priest.

Suddenly the horse began to slow down. My grandpère cracked the whip frantically a couple of times, but the horse, he jest keep goin' slow. My grandpère realized that the horse was pullin' hard, like there was a great weight on the sleigh. The horse was sweatin' and strainin' and so my grandpère turned around to see what was wrong, and there was a large black wolf hanging on to the back of the sleigh with his forepaws. Grandpère knew at once it was a loup-garou, 'cause no regular wolf would be pulling against the horse so strong and so determined-like.

My grandpère was real mad at that loup-garou for keepin' him from reachin' the priest. But he was more scared than mad, especially when that loup-garou jumped right into the sleigh with him and leaned his heavy forepaws on my grandpère's shoulders. Now that the weight was gone, the horse, him bein' as scared of the loup-garou as was my grandpère, he run like the Devil was on his heels.

The loup-garou was pushing down on my grandpère's shoulders till he thought he would be crushed. Grandpère was tryin' to reach his knife so he could prick the loup-garou and turn him back into a man. But he couldn't find his knife on account of his hands were tremblin' so hard 'cause he could feel the breath of the loup-garou against his neck and the fur of the loup-garou was brushin' his face. Grandpère was looking right into the terrible yellow eyes of the loup-garou, and he knew he was gonna be eaten, so he started praying aloud for Bon Dieu to save him.

Just then the horse ran through the priest's gate. Grandpère let out a yell, and the priest came running out of the house.

THE LOUP-GAROU

As soon as he saw the loup-garou, the priest said some word my grandpère didn't understand, and that loup-garou became a man right off and ran away into the woods. My grandpère, he fainted dead away, and it took the priest half an hour and a whole pint of whiskey to revive him.

When Grandpère came back to his house with the priest, Great-Grandpère was feelin' fit as a fiddle, so all that fuss was for nothin'.

35

Captain Paddock and Crookjaw

YARMOUTH, MASSACHUSETTS

Now way back about 1690 there was no greater whaler than Captain Ichabod Paddock. No sir! Even that famous whaling center, Nantucket, once sent for Captain Paddock so that he might instruct them in the fine art of whaling. The captain had slaughtered numerous cows and bulls in his time, but he jest about met his match in old Crookjaw.

Old Crookjaw was a behemoth of a sperm whale, battle-scarred and crook-jawed, who would make 200 barrels of oil if he made a thimble. And Crookjaw was the nemesis of Captain Paddock. The captain would let fly at that monstrous whale again and again with his iron, and that blasted iron would jest bounce off the whale's hide or shatter into a million pieces.

Captain Paddock spent several years chasing after Crookjaw with no success. Finally he decided that the whale was be-spelled by some foul witchcraft. He had heard about witches who traveled the sea in the bellies of whales, and he was determined to find out if Crookjaw was jest such a creature.

One day his ship spotted Crookjaw snoozing in the choppy waters of Handkerchief Shoal. The captain hove his ship to and pulled off his long-leggers. Plunging into the sea, he swam out

CAPTAIN PADDOCK AND CROOKJAW

to the whale's side and waited. When Crookjaw woke up, he gave a wide yawn. This was what the captain had been waitin' for. As soon as the whale's mouth was wide enough, he dived right in. It was a bit of a tight squeeze as he got deeper, but the captain saw a light ahead of him. Aha, thought he, and he pushed himself forward.

Suddenly Captain Paddock popped out into a snug, well-lit cabin with a table sittin' in the middle of the room. Facing each other across the table were the Devil and a very beautiful woman. Captain Paddock stared entranced at the woman, who

219

had golden hair, plum-blossom skin, and bewitching green eyes. The pair were playing cards, and they ignored the intruder.

Finally the Devil slammed his cards on the table. The cards were singed on the edges, and smoke rose from them as the Devil swore. "Again I lose a hand!" he said crankily. He kicked his chair and vanished in a puff of blue smoke.

Ichabod Paddock seized his chance to address the fair maiden. "I'm sorry, ma'am, fer interruptin' yer game."

The maiden laughed, her voice sounding like the waves lapping the seashore. "The game was over," she said merrily. "And I won."

Emboldened by her tone, Ichabod Paddock asked: "And what were the stakes?"

The woman gave him a bold look from her deep green eyes and said: "The stakes were for possession of you." She gave him a suggestive smile and said: "Come, sir. I have won, as you can plainly see. You must now oblige me."

Captain Paddock made no protest as she drew him deeper into the cabin.

By dawn the next mornin', the crew aboard his ship had given the captain up for lost. They were preparin' to leave when the waters of Handkerchief Shoal began to stir and Captain Paddock came swimmin' up to the ship.

After that, Captain Paddock went swimmin' each night at dusk and did not return until dawn, to the complete bewilderment of his crew. Like one be-spelled, he made little effort at whaling and grew pale and dreamy-eyed. After completing two such voyages in this manner, the captain began losing his grand reputation, and every man who shipped with him thought him completely balmy.

When the captain returned ashore after his second trip, his fair young wife gave him a shiny new whaling iron as a gift. For the first time in many days, Ichabod Paddock felt a stirring of the old whaling fever, not to mention a few pangs of guilt when he thanked his wife for such a generous gift. He was less pleased when she insisted he take her father along with him on his next voyage.

After a few days at sea, Crookjaw made an appearance off the port bow. The whale considered the captain and his vessel good friends by now and came close enough for the captain's father-in-law to get a good look at him.

"What a fish! What a fish!" his father-in-law shouted excitedly. "What are we waiting for? Lower fer him, Ichabod."

To refuse would have given away his nighttime escapades, so Ichabod reluctantly agreed, hopin' the whale would understand his game. After all, irons refused to pierce his skin. The two men went over in the small boat, and Paddock heaved his shiny new iron at Crookjaw. To his complete astonishment, he made fast. The huge whale thrashed and churned up the water somethin' fierce, and then died.

Captain Paddock was in a terrible state when they cut the whale open. What would he do when they found the cabin and its occupant? But inside the whale, where his cozy cabin for two had once resided, was only a golden piece of seaweed, a plum-blossom-colored shell, and two round sun-squalls as green as emeralds.

Followin' the death of Crookjaw, Captain Ichabod Paddock soon regained both his color and his reputation as a whaler. His wife never told him that the whaling iron she gave him was made from silver, the only metal capable of piercing the heart of a sea witch.

36

The Brick Wall

BOSTON HARBOR, MASSACHUSETTS

There is something very satisfying in the moment when I thrust the tip of my sword into the lying, cheating soldier's heart and watch him fall to the sandy ground outside the walls of Fort Independence, where I currently hold the post of captain. It is a clean blow that will take his life in a few hours. (I am nothing if not an expert swordsman.) Lieutenant Massey writhes a bit at my feet in the chill air of Christmas morning, just before losing consciousness. A job well done, I decide with a little nod, as I turn away from the dying man. The world will be a cleaner place without Robert Massey in it.

As the seconds cluster around the lieutenant, I clean my sword and sheath it. Then I walk away without looking back. Why should I soil my eyes further with the likes of Massey, a man who squeaked by on his charm and then cheated honest soldiers at cards? Good riddance to bad rubbish.

I enjoy the rest of the Christmas season on the base, in spite of the enmity displayed to me by the more common soldiers after Robert Massey dies. They had obviously been fooled by his charm. But not I. I can see through charm to the heart of a man. I pride myself on my ability and feel it is my duty to rid the world of the cheats and liars who worm their way into the military. I have dueled to the death with six other specimens as nasty as this one in the past and anticipate that I will do so again in the future, the world being as corrupt as it is.

The men under my command seem depressed in the weeks following the holiday, and I work them hard. They mention Massey frequently, and to my disgust a monument to the lying lieutenant is commissioned, to be erected upon the spot where he died. I complain but am overruled by my pig-headed superiors.

I retreat to my chambers to sulk and am soon joined by a delegation of my men. Friends of Massey, all, I think they have come to complain about the duel we fought. I am surprised and delighted to learn, instead, that they have come to their senses and now see the lieutenant for the liar and cheat he really was. We share a round of drinks and laugh together over their mistake. One drink leads to another until even I, who am famed for my tolerance of strong alcohol, am feeling rather tipsy.

The other soldiers are worse off than I, of course, and someone suggests as a lark that we explore the lower dungeons. An odd fancy, that, but one that I find alluring after consuming a few more drinks. Everyone sets off in merry spirits, drinking and singing and laughing, our voices echoing through the narrow passages. Deeper and deeper we go, and I suggest we search for phantoms along the way. The men cheer and begin making spooky noises that seem appropriate to the dark and dusty paths we are traveling.

In spite of my good head for spirits, my head is spinning and my legs feel like rubber. I sag a little, and one of the good ol' chaps supports me. I am surprised to see that it is Massey's best friend, but am in too happy a mood to wonder for long. He smiles as we stagger along and sings the words of a bawdy song with me. Another of Massey's cronies grabs my other arm when I trip, and the three of us chant together, to the amusement of the other men.

Things go a bit dim for me at this point. I am afraid I might even have passed out from too much drink—how embarrassing. When I come to, I am lying on my back in one of the dim old dungeons. After a moment, I realize that my wrists and ankles are shackled to the floor. Obviously another lark of some kind, I think, yanking against my restraints.

"Very funny, lads," I call out, turning my head toward the sound of voices and activity at the entrance to the cell. "Now set me free."

The soldiers don't answer me. A moment passes, then two. Then Massey's best friend appears holding mortar and a mason's trowel, and the other men begin handing him bricks. I realize that the soldiers are bricking up the entrance to the cell in which I lay shackled. "Very funny," I say again, louder this time. "Are you trying to teach me a lesson, lads? Is that what this trick is about? Make me sorry that I fought the duel with Massey? Because I'm not."

No one answers me. They work in silence, laying brick after brick until one row is done, then two. They are playing a game with me, of course. It is only a joke, I think. But something in the men's silence, in the way they build the wall more and more quickly, in the way they watch me with eyes that gleam in the dim light of the lantern, makes the hair stand up on my head and brings shivers to my body. If this is a joke, it is a nasty one.

Massey's best friend pauses in his work and looks directly into my eyes. At this moment I realize that this joke is no joke. The soldiers mean to bury me alive in this dungeon. I scream then, tugging hard at the shackles that bind me. Scream after scream rips from my throat as I struggle against my bonds. I hope that my screams will be heard by others who will come and rescue me. But this dungeon is too deep within the fort, I fear. No one will hear. No one will come. I will be entombed alive and written off the books as a deserter.

They are on the final row of bricks. I am reduced to bribery now, but no one speaks. No one heeds me. As the last few bricks are mortared into place, I begin to cry like a pitiful baby and beg the men to spare me this terrible fate. No one answers.

I watch in heart-thudding horror as the last brick is put in place, as the last chink of light fades from my sight. Then I am in utter darkness. I howl in panic, writhing against the iron manacles binding hands and feet and twisting my body this way and that in a frenzy, trying to get free before it is too late—although somewhere in my mind, I know that it is already too late. Eventually I fall back against the floor, spent by my thrashings. My wrists and ankles are wet with my own blood, and the pain of the split skin is an agony almost as deep as that within my mind.

My fingers are torn and throbbing from their intense scrabbling against the hard floor. My mind rails against the darkness, against the utter heartlessness that has trapped me here alive. I find myself weeping angrily, though I have never shed a tear in my lifetime. My lifetime, which can now be counted in hours. Hours! "Oh, God, save me," I whimper. But if my fellow soldiers have not offered me mercy, then how can God?

THE BRICK WALL

The agony of the thought sends me writhing again in spite of the horrible pain racking my wrists, ankles, and hands. Daylight. I must see daylight again. One more time. Just once more.

"Don't leave me here to die alone! Don't leave me!"

My voice echoes again and again in my ears, growing fainter as within me a terrible thirst grows. Water. I crave water, but there is no one to give me a drink. No one.

I am alone, and the sheer brutal horror of it overwhelms me more than the terrible thirst growing in my mouth and throat, and the throbbing pain of my self-inflicted injuries. My eyes strain against the complete and utter darkness, and I wonder if they are even open. The world inside my mind has dimmed, and it is only at greater and greater intervals that sheer terror arouses me from my stupor and makes me writhe in agony against the chains.

Dear God, *I can't get out. I can't get out. I CAN'T GET OUT!*

37

Elixir of Life

BENTON, NEW HAMPSHIRE

I remember Thomas when he was still a youth in school. Both of us were born and raised in Benton, but Thomas was several years older than me. I was still a chubby, red-cheeked little chap sitting in the front row under the eye of teacher when Thomas was taking his final exams. He was a bright young man, and folks in town banded together to get him a good start in life. He was going to study medicine and become the local doctor.

Just after I entered university, Thomas returned home with a bright, shiny new medical degree. He set up a practice in town and became a favorite among the eligible ladies throughout the county. We had a nodding acquaintance with one another, though I was only in town on holidays between classes.

Thomas and I only had one serious conversation during this period. During a Christmas Eve dance, we were partners in a card game and spent an enjoyable hour swapping stories about the strange habits of university professors. As the card game drew to a close, I told a story about my history professor, who had a pet pig that he brought to chapel with him every Sunday. Thomas countered with the tale of a German professor who was trying to achieve immortality by discovering the elixir of life. We both laughed at this exercise in futility. Thomas said: "It obviously did not work, for the professor died just before I graduated. He left me a trunk full of his research notes in his will. I have it tucked away in the attic, just in case I need to achieve immortality!" We were both still chuckling when my girl hauled me away to dance the next set with her.

In her frequent letters, my girl kept me informed of Thomas's many successes, both as a doctor and as a suitor. Eventually, Thomas became engaged to a very nice young woman from a rich family. The couple were due to wed the Christmas before I came home to work in the family business. But that summer, Thomas's fiancée contracted a severe case of typhoid fever and died in his arms. The whole county was struck by the tragedy, and it knocked the stuffing right out of the eligible young bachelor. After the funeral, Thomas packed up his belongings and retreated to a cabin on top of Mount Moosilauke, leaving the town without a doctor.

Later that year, my own courtship culminated in a lovely Easter wedding full of flowers, food, and family. I brought my lovely bride home to a nice house in Benton, where she reigned in splendor over me, our worldly goods, and a growing number of youngsters. Thomas was relegated to a sad memory, mentioned only in passing when someone complained about making the long trip two towns over to visit the doctor.

In autumn of 1824, just after we celebrated my baby daughter's second birthday, a new disease started killing all of the farm animals in the area. Cows and sheep would suddenly go missing and turn up dead. As the epidemic grew worse, even perfectly healthy horses suddenly died in their stalls. The local vet could find nothing wrong with the animals. The only common element was a strange wound that appeared behind each animal's left ear.

I saw one of the diseased animals when I took my family to my brother-in-law's house for supper one evening. My brother-in-law had found his mare dead in her stall just before dinner. Behind her left ear was a large red swelling with a white spot at the center.

"It looks like someone pricked her with a needle," I said uneasily, tilting the lantern so it shed more light on the wound.

For some reason, my brain presented me with the image of a long sharp needle akin to the ones I'd seen in the county doctor's office when we took our baby daughter to be treated for a fever. A physician's needle might very well leave such a wound behind. I didn't know of any natural cause that could produce such a wound.

I was quiet over supper, pondering the local mystery. Was someone using a stolen doctor's needle to prey upon local animals? But why would they do so? There was no pattern to it. Animals up and down the county were victims of this so-called disease, and their owners had nothing in common that would explain such a nasty campaign against them.

It wasn't until a corpse was stolen from an undertaker's wagon that I thought of Thomas. Medical students sometimes stole bodies to use in their research. But Thomas had given up his medical practice and lived as a hermit up on the mountain. Why would he need a body for research? Multiple bodies for medical research, I realized suddenly, could very well explain the rash of animal deaths last fall.

Then I remembered the story of the German professor who had devoted himself to the quest for eternal youth and left his notes on the elixir of life to Thomas. A horrible picture presented itself inexorably to my mind: a grieving Thomas packing up his belongings after the death of his beloved fiancée and coming across notes on eternal life from his former professor. This hypothesis seemed so plausible that I found myself confiding my theory to the sheriff the next day during my lunch hour. Then I went to the local mercantile to inquire after the erstwhile doctor-turned-hermit, who sometimes shopped there.

The owner of the mercantile leaned on the long counter, happy to chat while his wife conducted business with their customers. "We see Thomas every couple of months," he said. "He comes to town for supplies. Doesn't talk much. He looks kind of wild now: long premature gray hair, long black cape. Not someone you'd like to meet after dark, if you get my meaning." He paused thoughtfully. "A couple months ago, some loggers stopped by his cabin to see if he'd help one of their friends with a bad infection in his leg, but Thomas wasn't home. The loggers said the cabin was full of medical devices, dripping tubes, and mysterious things in bottles. Papers written in a spidery handwriting with hand-painted symbols in the corners spilled out of a large trunk by the fireside chair. It was very strange. The loggers were glad to get out of the place."

At that moment the undertaker's young son rushed in, breathless, and dragged me off to the funeral parlor. I found the sheriff in the back room with the undertaker. They'd found the missing corpse in the bushes near the town of Warren. Beside it was a second corpse, identity unknown. Both dead bodies had a pinprick behind the left ear.

"I think we need to talk with Thomas," I told the sheriff grimly. He agreed.

A group of us hiked up the mountain the next morning to the place where Thomas built his cabin. It was a desolate place with a rather precarious air, heightened by the presence of heavy cables anchoring the cabin to the rocks near the summit. The building looked as if it might fall off the mountain at any moment. The windows were dirty, no smoke came from the chimney, and the door was ajar. The cabin looked deserted.

We called a greeting. When no one responded, the sheriff pushed through the open door and entered the house. No one was there. Aside from a few sparse furnishings, it was empty. No food, no clothing, no medical equipment, no mysterious trunk full of papers. No elixir of life. Everything the loggers had seen a few months ago was gone. Thomas had vanished. After a thorough but fruitless search of the mountaintop, we made our way home in a thoughtful frame of mind.

As deep winter closed in, things settled down. No more animals died. No corpses went missing. It seemed like Thomas had gone for good. Then, just before spring, a hunter passing through town reported seeing a mysterious man with long gray hair and a black cloak at the far side of a clearing on the mountain. The mystery man vanished without speaking, and the hunter couldn't properly track the man's footsteps in the melting snow.

As the world greened again, stories of an alarming nature began circulating through the county. The rumors claimed that babies from nearby towns were disappearing from their cradles while they slept. The sheriff and I investigated the rumors, but no one we corresponded with had personal knowledge of an infant kidnapping. Still, the stories persisted through the summer and early fall. Mothers all over the county—my wife included—were in a continuous state of panic. Children were kept in the yard. Doors and windows were barred night and day. Everyone was crabby and exhausted from staying on high alert for so long.

Snow came early to the mountain that year. By November I was wearing my winter cloak and snow boots to the office each day. I was deep into my paperwork one afternoon when my eldest son threw open the door without knocking and shrieked: "Papa! Come quick! A man with long white hair and a black cloak just snatched the baby from the carriage while Mama was hanging the wash in the yard."

My heart leapt into my throat, and I broke out in a cold sweat. I grabbed my cloak and raced out the door before any coherent thought had entered my brain. My eldest daughter had summoned the sheriff, and the neighborhood women were comforting my sobbing wife as a group of us followed the man's footprints through the snow. Soon we left the town behind us and started climbing up the mountain. All I could think of was my precious baby daughter, who was only three years old. I would hunt Thomas to the ends of the earth if I had to, and when I found him . . .

The tracks led us through Little Tunnel Ravine into a box canyon, where they stopped abruptly. There was no way out of the canyon. Where had Thomas gone? Where was my baby girl? Suddenly, we heard maniacal laughter float down from above. We looked up and saw Thomas at the top of the cliff, white hair and black cloak tossed by a fierce wind. In his arms he cradled my little girl. He must have climbed the cliff one-handed, I thought numbly, staring in heart-palpating fear at my daughter.

"Don't hurt her," I pleaded through numb lips. "Please, Thomas, don't hurt her. Put her down."

ELIXIR OF LIFE

"Steady, friend," the sheriff murmured, stepping forward to address the miscreant. "Release the little one, Thomas, and it will go easier with you," he shouted up to the mad doctor.

I edged forward until I was standing right beside the cliff face, just below Thomas. I think I had some insane idea that I could climb the sheer rock wall and snatch my child from his hands.

"Release her, Thomas, please," I begged, staring up into his wild eyes. "You don't need to kill a child to find the elixir of life."

Thomas twitched and I swear his eyes glowed red in the late autumn dusk. "Yes, I do," Thomas shouted. And then he threw my daughter off the cliff. Her tiny body flew right over my head. I heard her little voice screaming as she fell. I whipped around, my eyes never leaving my child. I lunged after her plummeting body, my arms extended to their full length, my feet leaving the ground as I stretched every muscle, every sinew to catch my baby.

Every man in the search party ran forward, reaching out. But Thomas had judged the trajectory with insane intelligence. He threw my baby into the one empty spot in the box canyon. The folds of her dress brushed my extended fingertips as she fell the final six feet and landed with a terrible thud on the hard, snow-covered ground. A second later my own plummeting body slammed into the ground beside her.

We both slid several feet in the slippery snow as my arms wrapped a moment too late around my baby girl. I clutched her frantically to my chest. Her little body was crushed and broken, like my heart. I lay with my face buried against her dress, waiting to feel a breath that did not come, wishing that it was me who had died and not her. It should have been me.

I don't remember much after that moment. I don't remember the men climbing up the cliff to pursue the vanished Thomas. I don't remember walking down the mountain, carrying my dead little girl to my grief-stricken wife. I don't remember that they kept a suicide watch on both of us that night as we sat in the parlor with our dead baby. I barely remember the funeral.

But my wife and I had to pull ourselves together for the sake of our other three children, and so we did. It was the second hardest thing I've ever done. The first was putting my baby girl into a casket and burying her in the cold, hard ground.

They never found Thomas. He vanished like smoke after that night. Part of me rages that my daughter's murderer got away. Another part of me hopes he never returns. I think I would kill Thomas with my bare hands if I ever saw him again, and then I too would be condemned for murder. I couldn't do that to my poor, suffering family.

Over the years, a hunter or a woodsman will drop into the mercantile to report a sighting of a mysterious figure with long white hair and a black cloak haunting the mountain. They aren't sure if it is a man or a ghost, for he vanishes whenever they approach. For the sake of my family, I have never gone to investigate the story.

38

The Devil's Hole

WOONSOCKET, RHODE ISLAND

Long ago, back when my grandpère was young, there was no curé in our parish. No, not a one. The good people, they had to go to town for Easter, or to be married, or to have their children baptized. Driving to town was inconvenient for most of the year, for the roads were bad and often filled with mud. But the curé from town would travel those terrible roads once every fortnight to say Mass for all the poor folk in our parish. The farmers were so grateful for this kindness that they put up a small wooden chapel for the curé where he could hold services.

Our parish was a very poor place in those days, and there were not many people in it. But more and more families were arriving. Some would move right into the forest and begin clearing trees so they could farm. *Mon Dieu*, they were poor. They lived in small log houses and could afford no livestock. And the work was hard. They had to root out every stump and stone to make the soil ready for the plow. But people had expected life to be hard, and they knew that no one would do them any favors. So it was with surprise and great joy that they learned one day that they were to have a curé of their own.

When Monsieur le Curé came, there was no house for him, and no church. A good farmer and his wife took him in while the men built him a small shack in which to live. *Mon Dieu*, today the poorest of the poor would not suffer themselves to live in such a house. But Monsieur le Curé was a true saint. He had no false pride, and he was happy in his new parish.

Still, the people wanted more for their parish and for their good curé, so they decided to build a church. Monsieur le Curé was pleased with their noble idea, but troubled because the work of hauling stone was backbreaking without a horse, and there were no horses to spare. He was pondering ways and means one night in his small shack when, out of thin air, he heard someone call him by name. At once he was overcome by a great fear. But when he heard his name again, the fear left him and he remembered that he was in a state of grace.

"In the name of le Bon Dieu, tell me who you are and what you want," said the curé.

The figure of a beautiful White Lady appeared in the shack.

"Fear not, François," she said gently. "I am the Holy Virgin, and I have come to offer you a gift. Tomorrow you will find a horse tied beside your door. You shall use this horse to cart the stone for the church that the good people of this parish wish to build. The horse is very strong and will be able to carry the heaviest load you give him. But you must never take off the horse's bridle, for it is sanctified. If you remove the bridle, the horse will disappear forever."

Then the Holy Mother blessed him and vanished from his sight. Monsieur le Curé was left trembling in awe, tears rolling down his cheeks. Slowly he made ready for bed, but it took him a long time to sleep.

When he awoke the next morning, he thought the vision was a dream, until he heard a snort from outside his door and the sound of a horse pawing the ground. Running to the window, Monsieur le Curé saw a horse standing in his tiny garden, tied to the post by the house. It was a magnificent animal, pitch black in color, tall, sleek, and rippling with muscle. Two, three times the curé passed his hand over his eyes to make sure he was not dreaming.

Finally he went out his door and laid his hand on the horse's neck. The horse was real. The vision had come true. Monsieur le Curé studied the animal. It had a wicked gleam in its black eyes. The bridle of which the Virgin Mary had spoken was quite plain. But when he studied it closely, it seemed to glitter in the sunlight, as if its sanctity were being tested at every moment.

When the workmen arrived at five o'clock to begin hauling stone for the new church, Monsieur le Curé presented them with the horse.

"This horse is on loan from a friend," he told them. "He is a good horse, but is a bit wild. My friend has instructed me that this horse shall not be unbridled at any time, even when he eats or drinks, because he will run away."

"What is the name of this horse, Monsieur le Curé?" asked Louis Jarrett.

Monsieur le Curé hesitated for a moment. "I call him Old Nick," he said at last, looking for a moment into the black horse's eyes. "I am entrusting him into your care, Louis."

"I will take good care of him, Monsieur le Curé. But it seems an odd sort of name for such a horse." Louis shook his head. "Well, no matter. As long as Old Nick isn't possessed by the Devil, it will be all right."

"I will answer for him," Monsieur le Curé said with a tiny smile. "Just you keep his bridle on."

The men harnessed Old Nick to the cart and put in a regular load of stone. Old Nick hauled that load as if there were nothing in the cart. Monsieur le Curé, who was watching, told them not to worry about Old Nick. He could handle much heavier loads. So they piled in more stone. Old Nick didn't seem to notice any difference. He stepped as tall and proud as if he weren't pulling a cart full of heavy stone. The men were impressed. They sent someone to fetch a larger cart. This cart they filled with so much stone it resembled a load of hay. The stone was so heavy that the wheels cracked. Old Nick didn't even break a sweat.

A large crowd gathered that first day to watch Old Nick haul stone. No one had ever seen such a horse before. Not a speck of white could be found on him. He was a massive horse, more than eighteen hands, with an arched neck and a mane nearly down to his knees. But his eyes were wild, and Monsieur le Curé kept repeating his warning to stay away from Old Nick's mouth. Since the men didn't need to unbridle Old Nick, it was easy to heed the warning.

In the days that followed, the men hauled so much stone that the plans for the church were moved up. From time to time Monsieur le Curé would ask Louis how he liked Old Nick.

"He's a grand horse," Louis always said. "But I still think it's a curious name, Monsieur."

Louis was the only one allowed to drive Old Nick. But one day Louis could not come, and so Batisse Champlain replaced him. What can I tell you about Batisse? Oh, he was a good fellow and a hard worker. But *Mon Dieu*, he had a swelled head. Batisse was always boasting how his cow gave only cream, his

THE DEVIL'S HOLE

pigs were the fattest in the town, his wife made the best pancakes in the whole region, and his horse—words could not describe his horse!

Batisse was a hard fellow to listen to for long, but he was well known as a champion horse jockey, and he'd had his eye on Old Nick for quite a while. Batisse often criticized Louis's handling of the beast—behind his back, of course, and never in front of the curé. He was much pleased with this chance to drive such a magnificent horse. He boasted proudly to the other workmen, calling the horse "my Old Nick" until you would have thought he owned him.

Now, Louis had warned Batisse not to unbridle Old Nick. But Batisse had laughed at the man and said: "Don't you worry, Louis. I have bridled and unbridled many a horse, and if I wish to unbridle Old Nick, only the Devil could prevent me from bridling him again."

Louis, remembering the curé's words to him on the first day, said: "He just might, Batisse."

But Batisse only laughed.

Batisse enjoyed himself mightily, driving back and forth with Old Nick. They were drawing stone from the far side of the river, and the day was very hot. Toward noon Batisse stopped right in the middle of the river to get himself a drink. While he drank his fill, Batisse watched Old Nick. The horse stood still and did not even bend his head toward the water, despite the heat of the day. Batisse tried to force the horse to drink, but to no avail. "This is on account of that bridle," the man said. "The poor horse would drink if I took the bridle off. What do priests know about horses anyway?"

So saying, he laid one hand on the horse's long mane to hold him and with the other unbuckled the bridle and removed it. Well, Old Nick gave one great shake, and was gone like lightning, leaving harness and cart behind and Batisse lying fifteen feet away in the middle of the river. Old Nick was racing up the road as fast as he could go, when he saw Monsieur le Curé, who was on his way to visit a sick man. When Monsieur le Curé saw Old Nick, he placed himself in the middle of the road and drew the sign of the cross in the air.

Old Nick reared up and threw himself away from the curé. Leaving the road entirely, the horse sprang onto a rock overhanging the river. There was a thunderous noise and the rock split in two, making a cleft that was six feet wide and led to a deep cavern into which Old Nick disappeared.

Monsieur le Curé was quite upset at the loss of Old Nick. Knowing who and what the horse was, he had never cared for the beast, but without him the work of building the church was much harder on the people. Batisse Champlain was a much humbler man after the curé was done with him.

Now, Old Nick, who really was the Devil, was terribly insulted by his treatment in our parish, drawing stones for the building of a church not being to his taste. So the Devil set some evil spells on that cavern by the river, and it became known as the Devil's Hole. Any Christian who passed the Devil's Hole would find that his horse went lame or that his wheel broke or that some other misfortune befell him. Animals avoided the Devil's Hole, and any horse that went past trembled and started as if it sensed a terrible presence within. Moans and horrible screams came from the hole at night, and several times a huge black wolf was seen coming out of the cavern with flames spouting from its mouth. Only when Monsieur le Curé walked past was the Devil's Hole silent, its spells made as nothing before the priest's holiness.

For many long years the Devil's Hole plagued the people. After Monsieur le Curé's passing, many other priests came to our parish. Each one tried his best to end the Devil's sorceries. Some used holy water, others hung crosses. Services were held, candles lit, prayers said. Nothing did any good.

Then a new priest came, one very like in mind and attitude to the first curé. One night the Virgin Mary came to him in a dream and told him to erect a cross on the rock to end the evil deeds of the Devil. The next morning the new curé spoke to the men of the parish. The men gathered the very best wood and stone and supplies and carried them to the rock. Together the people made a cross and set it upon the rock beside the Devil's Hole. Then the curé consecrated the cross, sprinkling it with holy water and saying prayers. Everyone wept and repented and the men promised not to swear or drink.

And since that day, the Devil has never returned to the cavern.

39

Death Light

CAPE ELIZABETH, MAINE

Dear Emma,

The evening light's slowly fading through the windowpane. I reckon by the time the sun goes down, I will be dead and good riddance to me. You've thought me dead all these long years, wife, and so this letter will come as a shock to you. But I owe you an explanation for my behavior, and this is my last chance to confess. I've done you wrong twice, wife. Leaving you to think I was dead was the second wrong. The first wrong I did you was far worse.

I've loved your beautiful self just about forever, Emma. I followed you around the schoolyard when we were children, and when we grew up a bit I'd sit in my boat fishing and dream about taking you to the local dances and maybe sweeping you off your feet. You were in my thoughts every moment of every day, but I was too shy to tell you how I felt. I was just a poor fisherman's boy, and you were the gruff harbormaster's only daughter.

It was only after your Pa died in a storm that I felt as if things became equal between us. I started calling on you twice a week, steady as can be. I was just one of many local boys who were buzzing around your widowed Ma's place in those days, but I thought I was your favorite. We could always laugh together, and I thought that was a good sign.

Then one day I was walking up the shore from my boat with a mess of cod I'd caught for you and your widowed Ma, and I saw you leaning against the trunk of a big old fir tree in the side yard kissing Jack Welsh. Right then and there, the bottom dropped out of my world. I knew Jack was courting you, but I never dreamed you would like him better than me.

Love does funny things to a body. After that day, every time I saw Jack Welsh the world got red around the edges and I could barely breathe. I hated him so fiercely I wished him dead and crawling with maggots six feet under the churchyard. I cursed him every morning when I rose and every night when I went to bed. And every hour in between.

Late one evening at the dark of the moon, I saw Welsh alone beside his boat pulling in one of his crab traps. The whole world went red and dark around the edges. I trembled with rage, remembering the kiss beside the old fir tree. I grabbed a big chunk of driftwood that had swept up against a rock, crept up behind him, and hit him over the head. With a grunt, Welsh fell face down into the lapping waves, his skull crushed and blood flowing into the water. I brought my boat to the spot where he lay partially submerged, dragged him in, and sailed out into the night-darkened bay to dump his body into the ocean. Good riddance.

It was a nine days' wonder, the disappearance of Jack Welsh. You were pale and thin for a while after he vanished, but my frequent visits and gifts eventually put the smile back on your face. We got married on the anniversary of Jack Welsh's death, though you can be sure I never shared that tidbit with you.

We were on our way down to Boston for our honeymoon trip on that first anniversary, so we didn't see the death light that appeared out in the bay, sailed over to the dock where Welsh kept his boat, and then floated to your Ma's place to hover over the tree where I saw you kissing Jack. It vanished with a grunt, the sound a dying man might make after he was hit over the head with a piece of driftwood.

We moved in with your widowed Ma when we came home from our honeymoon, and we were real happy that first year. Then one night I woke from a bad dream, and I swear I saw Jack's face pressed against our bedroom window, which looked out over the harbor. I gave a yelp that woke you up, and I had to make up an excuse for my jitters. It happened again the next night and then the next. It didn't stop until we traded bedrooms with your Ma, since her window faced inland.

A week later, the death light made its second annual appearance in the center of the bay, paused on the shore where Jack died, and then came to hover over our house. Everyone in the settlement saw it. I felt as if I was wearing a brand that said "murderer." I was determined to move out of that haunted house. Fortunately, you and your Ma were so frightened by the death light that neither of you objected when I put the house up for sale the next day and moved us into a nice cottage on the far side of the inlet by the end of the week.

As if triggered by our move, the death light started appearing once a month at the dark of the moon. It popped into existence right over the place where I dumped Jack's body into the ocean, flew to the place where I hit him with the driftwood, and then made its way to the old house where we'd lived with your Ma. I felt as if the death light was looking for me, trying to figure out where I'd gone.

Everyone in our little community started talking about the mysterious light, which made me real nervous. Folks in the mercantile thought it might be your dead Pa come back to visit his old home, or maybe some other seafaring friend who wanted to look in on you and your Ma and didn't know you moved. The speculation was getting too close for my comfort. Every time the death light was mentioned, I pictured Jack bending over the crab trap and heard the grunt he made as he died.

After that, I made double and triple sure that I got home from fishing early enough to avoid any encounter with the death light. I didn't want Jack to find me again.

In August the Anderson boys and I got caught in a thick fog that prevented us from making it to shore before dark. It was very late when we pulled in. The

DEATH LIGHT

fog swirled across the wharf and blotted out the dark sky as we tied up the boat. Suddenly the mist split in two around us, leaving a strange open channel between our boat and the center of the bay. On either side of the channel, fog billowed and swirled in huge gray walls. Within the empty space, the dark ocean reflected thousands of stars back at the night sky.

Then the death light appeared in the middle of the cleared-out channel. It was an eerie blue-white ball of fire that reflected blindingly off the walls of fog on either side. The death light came hurtling toward the three of us. The Anderson boys yelped with fear and flopped facedown on the wharf. I threw myself back into the boat and crouched in the bottom with my arms protectively over my head as the light honed in on my position. The ghost light darted around the boat, bouncing off the rigging. I swear I felt my hair sizzle as it hovered over my head. I refused to look up. As the eerie light pressed down on me, I saw Jack's dead face in my mind. It was dripping with blood from the terrible crushed skull. I heard the dying grunt he made as he fell.

After a moment, the light rushed away from me. I uncurled my trembling body and lunged for the side of the boat to see where it went. The death light hovered over the place where I'd murdered Jack, several hundred yards down the shore. I watched it float toward your Ma's old home like it always did. Then it paused and changed direction. My heart nearly stopped when the death light came to rest over the roof of our new cottage. Jack Welsh may as well have hung a sign on our front door: "My murderer lives here."

The Anderson boys were still trembling facedown on the wharf and didn't notice where the death light had gone. But someone in the community was bound to notice and ask questions.

As soon as the death light vanished, I hightailed it home, packed a bag, and left. You asked me where I was going, but I couldn't tell you. I didn't know myself. You wanted to know when I'd be home, and I couldn't tell you that either. I just knew I had to go right away. Sooner or later, someone would figure out what that death light meant if I stuck around.

Dawn was breaking as I looked my last on our little house by the shore. A white figure stood by the gate watching my departure. It was the ghost of Jack Welsh. I knew then that I would never return. Jack had won you after all.

Your repentant husband,
Tom Wright

40

Madness

I watch in silent glee as the first seeds of madness are scattered onto the fertile ground of this place called Salem. . . .

It begins in 1689, when the new minister, Samuel Parris, moves into Salem Village with his family. They own a slave woman named Tituba. I study the slave with interest, for the secret tenets of her religion are dark indeed, and she believes them utterly. It is she who—unbeknownst to anyone—begins planting the seeds of destruction as she relates the stories of her people to the young ones. Such a small thing, and yet it will grow into a terrible storm come the spring of 1692.

I introduce myself immediately to the family, and soon I am considered a dear friend and an excellent Christian. Oh, yes, I chuckle inwardly, I am indeed an excellent Christian— outwardly! Soon I am taking tea with the minister's wife once a week, sitting before the fire and discussing church work. And quietly, I nurture the seeds of madness and watch them grow within the household.

In January of 1692 I make my customary visit to the minister's house for tea and talk. It is a fine winter day, and I sit sipping from my cup and watching little Betty Parris playing near the hearth. She drops her ball and it rolls into the hearth—too close to the fire. She stretches out her hand to retrieve it, and I say softly: "I wouldn't if I were you, my dear."

I tug on the handkerchief in my lap, pulling it toward me to cover the small gesture I make with my hidden hand. In front of me, little Betty's hand stops abruptly a few inches from the hot fire. She cries out in surprise, causing her mother to look over to see what is wrong. Seeing how close the child is to the fire, her mother gasps and pulls little Betty away from the hearth, sending her to the kitchen to sit with Tituba. I watch the little girl leave with a slight smile on my lips. I do not wish this particular child to be damaged in any way. No indeed. For I have looked into her eyes and seen the madness that has taken hold of her soul.

Just a few days later, Elizabeth comes to me with a frightened face and a disturbing story. Little Betty has been stricken with terrible convulsions, dashing about, diving under furniture, contorting in pain, and complaining of fever. The child has even screamed blasphemous words in the midst of her madness.

I am suitably shocked and take care not to speak of witchcraft. It is too soon to speak of this to Elizabeth Parris. But I drop hints to the other good folk in the village, priming the pump so that the madness will come gushing forth.

I possess a copy of that very useful book penned by Cotton Mather. It is called *Memorable Providences,* and it describes the suspected witchcraft of an Irish washerwoman in Boston. In a careful and discreet way, I bring the villagers' attention to the close parallel between Betty's behavior and that of the witchcraft victim described in the book. It goes down very well, and it is not long before the doctor himself believes the child is bewitched.

Soon, Little Betty's bizarre behavior spreads to encompass eleven-year-old Abigail Williams, Ann Putnam Jr., and other Salem girls. The girls contort into grotesque poses, fall down in frozen postures, and complain of biting and pinching sensations. "Witchcraft," some whisper. It does not take long for this rumor to spread. In just a few days, the populace is shouting the words aloud in the street: "The girls are bewitched."

I mention casually to Mistress Sibley, a neighbor of the afflicted Parris family, that something must be done to counter the enchantment. My hint is enough. Soon she conspires with Tituba to bake a rye cake made with the urine of the afflicted child and feed it to a dog, an old folk cure sure to help the girl. This un-Christian response to the problem focuses community attention on the slave woman who believes so strongly in the supernatural. Perhaps she is the answer to their problem.

Two days after the rye cake is baked, arrest warrants are issued against Tituba; Sarah Good, a social misfit; and Sarah Osborn, who has not attended church for a year. Two of the afflicted children—Betty Parris and Abigail Williams—name these three women as the source of their troubles, and they are believed.

The Putnam family, whose daughter Ann is among the afflicted seven, brings a complaint against the three women to county magistrates Jonathan Corwin and John Hathorne, who schedule examinations for the suspected witches on March 1, 1692, in Ingersoll's tavern.

On the day of the examination, hundreds of people arrive to watch the show. (Oh, dear, a slip of the tongue. I mean *the trial.*) The examinations are moved to the meetinghouse, where the girls describe the attacks made on them by the specters of the three women. When approached by the accused, the girls fall into contortions. Other villagers come forward with tales of deformed animals and the highly suspicious circumstance of butter and cheese gone bad after a visit by one or another of the women. The magistrates speak to the women, hammering them over and over with the same questions: Are you witches? Have you seen Satan? How, if you are not witches, do you explain the contortions caused by your presence? I am delighted by the performance. It is obvious that the magistrates think the women guilty as charged.

But it has not gone far enough for me. Not yet. The magistrates seem set on admonishing the women and letting them go. This will not do. I roll my handkerchief into a ball as I place a picture into the mind of Tituba. She is impressionable and breaks easily. A moment later, she tells the magistrates that she was once approached by a tall dark man who asked her to sign his book and do his work. The commotion this confession causes among the crowd is delightful to hear.

Soon Tituba gives way to lofty flights of imagination, claiming to fly through the air in the company of four other witches and claiming that the Devil blocks her whenever she tries to confess and repent of her sins to the good Reverend Parris. Her confession is the spark that sets the village aflame. Soon the local ministers are hunting for witches and finding them everywhere.

The night after the first trial, I spend an hour drawing the face of a village woman upon the bark of a tree. It is a good likeness of the woman, whom I hate. Rebecca Nurse slighted me many years ago, and I have never forgotten it or forgiven her. Now I take the picture and drop it into the stream, where the water will eat away at it until it is gone—and Rebecca Nurse with it.

Drunk with their newly perceived power, the "bewitched" girls start accusing more women of witchcraft. Their writhing antics are believed and more arrests ensue, including those of Martha Corey and Rebecca Nurse. One Sunday during church service, Ann Putnam suddenly shouts: "Look where Goodwife Cloyce sits on the beam suckling her yellow bird between her fingers!" This is taken as proof of Sarah Cloyce's guilt by many who hear the child's words. The girls even accuse the four-year-old daughter of Sarah Good of sending a specter to bite them. A foul accusation indeed, and even I am shocked when the child is arrested and put into prison. After all, we must preserve the future generation, or who will be left for us to dominate? I set a spell that night to make sure the girls will send no more children to prison.

The jails are filling up rapidly with accused witches, much to the delight of the girls and also, I see, local Sheriff Corwin, who is not above skimming a profit off the proceedings. Interesting.

The girls have enhanced their performances by this time. Sometimes, they pretend to be struck dumb by the witches who are tormenting them. Other times, they scream and writhe in agony and pretend to see visions. They are widely believed, and other villages send for the girls to discover if they too are plagued by witches. Strangely, all of them are—according to the little dears.

Some of the accused begin to "confess" to their crimes, fearing the gallows. This increases the fear and tension in all the towns surrounding Salem. By the time newly appointed Governor Phipps arrives from England, the jails are full, and the colony is in chaos.

Phipps creates a new court, the "court of oyer and terminer," to try the witchcraft cases, and he appoints to it five judges, including, I note, three close friends of Cotton Mather. At Mather's urging, the court admits spectral evidence, which is the testimony of the afflicted who claim to see the apparition or the shape of the person afflicting them. They also instigate the touch test, in which the accused are asked to touch the victims, it being assumed that the touch of a witch will stop the contortions of the afflicted. The court even has the accused examined for "witch marks"—moles thought to be created by the bite of a witch's familiar. Hearsay, gossip, unsupported assertions, surmises—all these and more become evidence against the accused, who are given no legal counsel, can have no witnesses testify on their behalf, and are not allowed to appeal a verdict.

Bridget Bishop, owner of a tavern, is the first brought to trial on June 2, 1692. She is also the first to die. Following her hanging, Justice Nathaniel Saltonstall resigns from the court in disgust, but I am relieved to see that this does not deter the bloodlust of the other justices, and Bridget Bishop's death is rapidly followed by others.

I wait impatiently for accusations to be made against Rebecca Nurse and finally push a vision of her into the minds of several of the afflicted girls. The next day, Rebecca Nurse is named a witch, and a trial follows shortly. To my surprise, both Ann Putnam Jr. and Ann Putnam Sr. accuse her of witchcraft.

MADNESS

No one heeds the fact that Nurse is a member of a Topsfield family that has had a long-standing quarrel with the Putnams.

To my fury, the Nurse jury returns a verdict of not guilty. But a few twists of my handkerchief turn the mind of Chief Justice Stoughton, who tells the jury to reconsider a statement of Nurse's that he considers an admission of guilt. The jury reconvenes and brings back a verdict of guilty. On July 19, 1692, Nurse rides with four other convicted witches to Gallows Hill.

The following week is enlivened by yet more histrionics by the girls. They writhe and contort, and little Betty Parris's eyes dart to and fro, seeking another victim. For a moment they land on me, gleaming. Calmly, I smile at her, and into her mind I say: "I wouldn't if I were you, my dear." Betty's eyes widen in shock and she screams in real agony as I give a small twist to the handkerchief in my lap, and red welts form upon her neck and face. She cowers back, her eyes sliding frantically from side to side. They land upon a woman in the next pew, a woman who was on the opposite side of her father in a recent congregational dispute, and little Betty screams her name aloud, pointing her free hand at the newly accused witch. "Good girl," I whisper into her mind, releasing the handkerchief and with it my spell. The red welts fade from her skin as if they had never been. I find it strange, as I watch Betty writhe on the meeting room floor, screaming the names of her tormentors, that the people of Salem see the Devil's handiwork everywhere but in the one place where it is most visible.

As the summer progresses, those who have scoffed at the trials, such as tavern owner John Proctor, become targets of the accusers. Ex-minister George Burroughs is dragged back from his home in Maine to face trial after Ann Putnam claims that he bewitched soldiers during a failed military campaign in the frontier war. Mercy Lewis tells the court that Burroughs flew her to the top of a mountain and, pointing toward the surrounding land, promised her all the kingdoms if only she would sign his book. When he is executed, Burroughs not only refuses to confess, but he recites the Lord's Prayer perfectly, something that the colony believes cannot be done by a witch. (How wrong they are!) The crowd is greatly moved, but the execution goes forward at Cotton Mather's behest.

I find it amazing that no one seems to notice that most of the accused are better off financially than the accusers, and that many of the accusing families stand to gain property from the convictions of accused witches. And, of course, many of the accusers sided against George Burroughs in the schism that split the church a few years back. But the witch-hysteria is so strong now that practical matters are brushed aside in favor of specters and bad luck and fanciful stories. And Sheriff Corwin collects fees, confiscates property, and delights in his power over his neighbors almost as much as the "afflicted" girls and their families.

One of the accused, an eighty-year-old man named Giles Corey, sees through the facade. Understanding the futility of a trial and knowing that the state will seize his farm if he is convicted of witchcraft, Corey remains mute when asked to lodge a plea with the court, hoping to preserve the family farm for his sons-in-law. The English penalty for such a refusal is *peine et fort*—death by pressing. It is torture—plain and simple—and involves piling heavy stones on top of the victim until the truth is "pressed" out of him (or he dies).

Corey is condemned to death. On September 19 he is stripped naked, pushed into a pit dug in the field behind the Salem jail, and his body pressed underneath heavy stones. Sheriff Corwin stands over the pit, asking the old man to confess, over and over. Corey says nothing, though more and more stones are piled upon him, making his eyes bulge and his tongue pop out of his mouth. Corwin pushes the tongue back in and keeps piling on stones. Corey dies two days later, cursing the sheriff and Salem with his last breath.

The whole town is shocked and subdued by the torture undergone by the old man. And still, the witch trials continue. Three days after Corey's death, on September 22, 1692, eight more convicted witches, including Corey's wife, are hanged.

It cannot last, of course. The Reverend John Hale begins to question the probability of so many prominent citizens embracing the Devil's work all at once, and even the foolish concede his point. Yet as I look at the greedy, gullible, vain faces of the accusing girls and their kinfolk, I believe the good reverend is wrong. It is possible for a large number of people to simultaneously embrace the Devil. In Salem, they are the accusers.

Then Increase Mather—father of devoted witch-hunter Cotton Mather—prints a tract arguing that it is better to let suspected witches escape than to kill the innocent. And, to my chagrin, a Bostonian minister named Samuel Willard writes another suggesting that the Devil himself might create the specter of an innocent person and parade it before the eyes of the afflicted. (A fact I would rather not have gotten out, since I myself have used this trick more than once.)

The opinions of these men sway the heart of the governor, who orders the court to exclude spectral evidence and touching tests. Without these, the trials are proved a sham. The girls continue with their accusations for a few months more, but reach too high when they accuse the governor's own wife of being a witch. Within a month of this accusation, the trials are shut down, and all the remaining accused are released from jail. And so the madness dies away at last, and the witch trials come to a bitter conclusion. According to my private records, nineteen convicted witches have been executed, four have died in prison, Giles Corey has been pressed to death, and between one and two hundred other people have been arrested and imprisoned on charges of witchcraft.

Life slowly returns to normal in Salem. Every Sabbath I walk silently through the churchyard, carrying my prayer book. Around me, the congregants are sober and exhausted, glad to see an end to the madness. I am sated for the moment by all the bloodshed and pain and anguish, but it will not be long before I crave more. I walk down the aisle and take my seat. Laying my prayer book in my lap, I piously turn my attention toward the altar where the minister calls us to worship. For countless generations, all the women in my family have been witches. And none of us have ever been caught.

Resources

Asfar, Daniel. *Ghost Stories of America*. Edmonton, AB: Ghost House Books, 2001.

Barber, John Warner. *Connecticut Historical Collections*. New Haven and Hartford: Clerk's Office of the District Court of Connecticut, 1836.

———. *Massachusetts Historical Collections*. Clerk's Office of the District Court of Massachusetts. Worcester, MA: Dorr, Howland and Company, 1839.

Battle, Kemp P. *Great American Folklore*. New York: Doubleday & Company, 1986.

Botkin, B. A., ed. *A Treasury of American Folklore*. New York: Crown Publishers, 1944.

———. *A Treasury of New England Folklore*. New York: Crown Publishers, 1965.

Boyd, Katie, and Beckah Boyd. *Ghosts of New Hampshire's Lakes Region*. Charleston, SC: Haunted America, 2010.

Brennan, John T. *Ghosts of Newport: Spirits, Scoundrels, Legends and Lore*. Charleston, SC: Haunted America, 2007.

Brunvand, Jan Harold. *The Choking Doberman and Other Urban Legends*. New York: W. W. Norton, 1984.

Carmer, Carl. *The Hurricane's Children*. New York and Toronto: Farrar & Rinehart, 1937.

Carter, Donald. *Connecticut's Seaside Ghosts*. Atglen, PA: Schiffer Publishing, 2008.

Citro, Joseph A. *Green Mountain Ghosts, Ghouls & Unsolved Mysteries*. New York: Houghton Mifflin Company, 1994.

———. *The Vermont Ghost Guide*. Lebanon, NH: University Press of New England, 2000.

———. *Vermont's Haunts*. Hertford, NC: Crossroad Press, 2012.

———. *Weird New England*. New York: Sterling, 2005.

Cody, Marie. "Woburn's Conservation Areas—Rag Rock." Waldenfont.com. Accessed February 22, 2003. www.waldenfont.com/wren/conservation_areas/ragrock.asp.

Coffin, T. P., and H. Cohen. *Folklore in America*. New York: Doubleday and AMP Company, 1966.

Cohen, Daniel, and Susan Cohen. *Hauntings & Horrors*. New York: Dutton Children's Books, 2002.

Cumerlato, Daniel. "Ghosts of the World—Emily's Bridge." Hauntedhamilton.com. Accessed February 27, 2003. www.hauntedhamilton.com/gotw_emilysbridge.html.

D'Agostino, Thomas. *Haunted New Hampshire*. Atglen, PA: Schiffer Publishing, 2006.

———. *Haunted Rhode Island*. Atglen, PA: Schiffer Publishing, 2006.

Digges, Jeremiah. *Cape Cod Pilot*. Provincetown and New York: Modern Pilgrim Press and the Viking Press, 1937.

———. *In the Great Waters*. New York: Macmillan Company, 1941.

Dorson, R. M. *America in Legend*. New York: Pantheon Books, 1973.

Drake, Samuel Adams. *A Book of New England Legends and Folk Lore*. Boston: Little, Brown and Company, 1883.

———. *The Heart of the White Mountains*. New York: Office of the Librarian of Congress at Washington, DC, 1881.

———. *The Myths and Fables of To-Day*. Boston: Lee and Shepard, 1900.

Earle, Alice Morse. *Stage-Coach and Tavern Days*. New York and London: Macmillan Company, 1900.

Editors of Life. *The Life Treasury of American Folklore*. New York: Time Inc., 1961.

Flanagan, J. T., and A. P. Hudson. *The American Folk Reader*. New York: A. S. Barnes & Co., 1958.

Flanders, Alice V. "The Story of Ocean Born Mary." Henniker.org. Accessed February 17, 2003. www.henniker.org/obmary.htm.

Greylock, Godfrey. *Taghconic: The Romance and Beauty of the Hills*. Boston: Lee and Shepard, 1879.

Hauck, Dennis William. *Haunted Places: The National Directory*. New York: Penguin Books, 1994.

Hazard, Thomas R., and Willis P. Hazard. *Recollections of Olden Times*. Rhode Island: Office of the Librarian of Congress at Washington, DC, 1879.

Hine, C. G. *The Story of Martha's Vineyard*. Office of the Librarian of Congress, Washington, DC. New York: Hine Brothers, 1908.

HollowHill.com. "The Disappointing Truth Behind the Ocean-born Mary 'Ghost Story.'" Accessed February 17, 2003. www.hollowhill.com/nh/oceanborn2.htm.

Johnson, Clifton. *New England and Its Neighbors*. New York: Macmillan Company, 1902.

Kuzmeskus, Elaine. *Connecticut Ghosts*. Atglen, PA: Schiffer Publishing, 2006.

Leach, M. *The Rainbow Book of American Folk Tales and Legends*. New York: World Publishing Co., 1958.

Leclair, William. *Manuscripts of the Federal Writers' Project of the Works Progress Administration for the State of Rhode Island*. Woonsocket, RI.

LiBrizzi, Marcus. *Dark Woods, Chill Waters: Ghost Tales from Down East Maine*. Camden, ME: Down East Books, 2007.

———. *Ghosts of Acadia*. Camden, ME: Down East Books, 2011.

Livermore, S. T. *Block Island*. Hartford, CT: Press of the Case, Lockwood & Brainard Company, 1882.

MacIntosh, Eibhlin. "Ocean-born Mary." Suite 101.com. Accessed February 17, 2003. www.suite101.com/article .cfm/spirits_magickal_and_mundane/31507.

Nason, Emma Huntington. *Old Hallowell on the Kennebec.* Augusta, ME: Loudon Hill, 1909.

Nelson, Joseph C. "The Gold Brook Bridge in Stowe." Vermontbridges.com. Accessed February 27, 2003. www.vermontbridges.com/goldbrk.htm.

Norman, Michael, and Beth Scott. *Historic Haunted America.* New York: Tor Books, 1995.

Peck, Catherine, ed. *A Treasury of North American Folk Tales.* New York: W. W. Norton, 1998.

Polley, J., ed. *American Folklore and Legend.* New York: Reader's Digest Association, 1978.

Revai, Cheri. *Haunted Connecticut.* Mechanicsburg, PA: Stackpole Books, 2006.

Robinson, J. Dennis. "The Truth About Ocean Born Mary." SeacoastNH.com. As I Please 5, no. 4. Accessed February 17, 2003. www.seacoastnh.com/arts/please042101.html.

Robinson, Rowland E. *Danvis Folks.* Boston and New York: Houghton Mifflin Company, 1894.

Rule, Leslie. *Coast to Coast Ghosts.* Kansas City, KS: Andrews McMeel Publishing, 2001.

Russell, Davy, ed. "Emily's Bridge." Xproject.com. Accessed February 27, 2003. www.xproject.net/archives/ paranormal/emilysbridge.html.

Schulte, Carol Olivieri. *Ghosts on the Coast of Maine*. Camden, ME: Down East Books, 1989.

SeacoastNH.com. "The Jonathan Moulton House." SeacoastNH.com. Accessed February 17, 2003. www.seacoastnh.com/arts/moulton1.html.

Skinner, Charles M. *American Myths and Legends*. Vol. 1. Philadelphia: J. B. Lippincott, 1903.

———. *Myths and Legends of Our Own Land*. Vols. 1 and 2. Philadelphia: J. B. Lippincott, 1896.

Smitten, Susan. *Ghost Stories of New England*. Auburn, WA: Ghost House Books, 2003.

Snow, Edward Rowe. *The Islands of Boston Harbor*. Andover, MA: Andover Press, 1935.

Standsfield, Charles A., Jr. *Haunted Maine*. Mechanicsburg, PA: Stackpole Books, 2007.

———. *Haunted Vermont*. Mechanicsburg, PA: Stackpole Books, 2007.

Sylvester, Herbert Milton. *Maine Pioneer Settlements: Old York*. Boston: W. B. Clarke Company, 1909.

Thaxter, Celia. *Among the Isles of Shoals*. Boston: Office of the Librarian of Congress at Washington, DC, 1909.

Thompson, D. P. *History of the Town of Montpelier*. Office of the District Court for the District of Vermont. Montpelier, VT: E. P. Walton, Printer, 1860.

Verde, Tom. *Maine Ghosts & Legends.* Camden, ME: Down East Books, 1989.

Vorse, Mary Heaton. *Time and the Town: A Provincetown Chronicle.* New York: Dial Press, 1942.

Witherspoon, Halliday. *Liverpool Jarge, Yarns.* Boston: Square Rigger Company, 1933.

Zeitlin, Steven J., Amy J. Kotkin, and Holly Cutting Baker. *A Celebration of American Family Folklore.* New York: Pantheon Books, 1982.

About the Author

S. E. Schlosser has been telling stories since she was a child, when games of "let's pretend" quickly built themselves into full-length stories acted out with friends. A graduate of the Institute of Children's Literature and Rutgers University, she created and maintains the website AmericanFolklore.net, where she shares a wealth of stories from all fifty states, some dating back to the origins of America. Sandy spends much of her time answering questions from visitors to the site. Many of her favorite e-mails come from other folklorists who delight in practicing the old tradition of who can tell the tallest tale.

About the Illustrator

Artist Paul Hoffman trained in painting and printmaking. His first extensive illustration work on assignment was in Egypt, drawing ancient wall reliefs for the University of Chicago. His work graces books of many genres—including, children's titles, textbooks, short story collections, natural history volumes, and numerous cookbooks. For *Spooky New England*, he employed a scratchboard technique and an active imagination.